More Missouri Ghosts

Fact, Fiction and Folklore

Joan Gilbert

Illustrations and Cover Art
by Adele Graham

Mogho Books LLC
Hallsville, MO

More Missouri Ghosts

Published by MoGho Books
P. O. Box 200
Hallsville, MO 65255

Printed and bound in the United States of America
by Modern Litho-Print Co.
First Edition
ISBN 0-615-11888-7

Library of Congress Catalog
Number 00 092004

Publisher's Cataloging-in-Publication Data
(Provided by Quality Books, Inc.)

Gilbert, Joan.
   More Missouri Ghosts: fact, fiction and
folklore / Joan Gilbert; illustrations and cover
art by Adele Graham. -- 1st ed.
   p. cm.
   Includes bibliographical references and index.
   LCCN: 00-92004
   ISBN: 0-615-11888-7

   1. Ghosts--Missouri. 2. Haunted places--
Missouri. 3. Parapsychology--Missouri.
I.Title.

BF1472.U6G54 2000   133.1'09778
              QBI00-500101

*Legends and yarns and folk-tales
are as much a part
of the real history of a country
as proclamations and provisions
and constitutional amendments.*

Stephen Vincent Benet

Acknowledgements and Dedication

So many people have helped in so many ways with this book that trying to list them all would be a hopeless undertaking. Therefore, the dedication is to:

everyone who helped, by their interest, to inspire doing the book;

everyone who, by taking it for granted that I could do the book made me take it for granted too;

everyone who shared an unexplainable experience;

everyone who sent clippings or photocopies;

everyone who, as part of their job with a library or newspaper, took the time to find material I requested;

particularly, everyone who helped me compute!

and especially fellow members of Missouri Writers' Guild and the Columbia Chapter;

most of all, everyone who buys the book and, I hope, enjoys it!

Table of Contents

Preface

The subtitle says it all, about this second collection of ghost stories presented for your pleasure. They range from fact — declared without reservation by some of those sharing experiences — to folklore to intentional fiction, and even a couple of poems. Some stories are long and detailed while others are short, offering essence only. Some are strongly tied to Missouri history and others belong to the present decade. More important, most were volunteered by readers of my earlier book, *Missouri Ghosts*.

I was amazed to see how many people find great fascination in the supernatural and how many can relate an unexplainable personal experience. The variety among these is remarkable and it does seem that if all data from Missourians were pooled, a few new insights might be gained. It would not be the first time that random observations of so-called ordinary people proved more significant than findings of researchers doing intensive long-term study.

I must admit, however, that more than a year's working with this material led me to no new revelation. It merely strengthened my conviction that humans have a lot to learn, in this area as in many others. I am now more certain than ever that contemptuous dismissal of what we do not understand is, as William James said, "bad method."

Joan Gilbert, June 30, 2000

More Missouri Ghosts

Basic
Ghosts

The most important question each of us has to answer is what happens to us after death. We don't want to accept it as finality. Ghosts are proof that there is a spirit inside that survives death.

John Carpenter, movie director

Chapter One

Apparitions

The figure was about my height, had blurred, milky-white features and a warm, friendly smile. I knew I should be scared, but I wasn't. Then slowly, very slowly, it reached out, as if to touch me.

Jim Longo, in his book, *Haunted Odyssey*

When we say "ghost" most of us are thinking of an entity like Longo's, something visible, usually something white and semi-transparent drifting about, maybe making faint gestures, maybe attempting to speak, maybe displaying horrible injuries. This is the common image, though serious students of the supernatural tell us that we often see ghosts without realizing it because they cannot be distinguished from a living person. We're told, too, that spirits can send messages gently into our minds, no physical manifestation necessary. We may regard their offerings as our own wit and wisdom, or as richly deserved inspiration.

Missouri apparitions are as varied as everything else in this state. Some seem quite conventional, like the mother who returned from the hereafter to guide her son and provide needed light on one of the most danger-fraught nights of his life. Other visible Missouri ghosts are unusual in the extreme, like those who pass right through the body of an observer, or allow an observer to pass through them. Since these instances are relatively few in the annals of parapsychology, we'll start with two of them.

Bob and Joanna Roller, now sheep farmers near Centralia, and Tim Lowery, who lives in the Kansas City area, became good friends while working at a large dairy farm near Independence, on Crenshaw Road, near the Little Blue River. In addition to sharing work, the three shared some ghostly experiences. Employees there had warned them that the farm was haunted. Some thought of the entity as an aging man, maybe a former owner of the dairy or a former employee. Some speculated that the manifestation came from times long before there was a dairy on the site. Stories as to what had actually been seen were vague, but this is that the three friends experienced.

Tim: "I would be conscious of something zipping by me, too fast to see, usually, making a sort of vibrating disturbance that was very unnerving. The few times I saw anything it was, to the best I can describe, an outline of a human figure, but filled in with black emptiness, space."

Bob: "I saw him in the dairy, sort of lurking in corners and corridors, always watching us, looking something like a person with a grey sheet draped over him. Once, out in the field, I saw him full body, dressed like a real person. I glanced momentarily to my equip-ment and when I looked up again, he was gone, but there was no place for him to go. I knew it was the same entity by his posture and the way he kept looking around."

Joanna: "We were provided a place to live, a big old two-story farm house. Several odd little things happened there, but my main event was seeing something streak through the rooms, looking like a person in dark draperies or maybe a gorilla costume, which made no sense at all. But there was a feeling of animality about it, strong movement of air, and a big bang just before we saw it." Her husband adds, "I thought somebody had broken the door in, knocking it to the floor."

It was Bob Roller who had a seeming ghostly walk-through. Tim, researching the supernatural, had decided to try to repel the haunt by projecting the strongest rejecting attitude toward it that he could muster. Roller felt this was a mistake, that it might inspire malignant reaction. Sure enough, when they next saw the ghost and Tim tried his experiment, the entity moved suddenly toward them in what seemed a menacing way.

Roller says he felt nothing when the being passed through his body except a slight chill and hair rising on his neck. "I was not afraid," Roller says. "It was very quickly over, and I was somehow not afraid. I knew I was not in danger, that he was leaving rather than attacking me." Roller's experience is quite different from a walk-through described in a novel called *Fog Heart*. Whether based on somebody's report or purely imaginary, that ghost's passage was devastating. The victim suffered a nosebleed and was left weak and nauseated, in her bed for a day.

The Rollers and Lowery never learned of anything in the history of the dairy that would explain what they saw and felt. They are not in touch with former co-workers, so don't know if the supernatural events have continued, or even whether the dairy still functions.

A Mirror Image

An interesting reversal of Bob Roller's experience came to St. Louisan Bevy Jaegers when she was just beginning to pursue the idea of becoming a psychic investigator. In her book, *Ghost Hunting, Professional Haunted House Investigators,* she recounts events of the first outing she and her husband, Ray, took with a local group of the curious. The evening's assignment was for individuals to explore separately in a decaying mansion and later pool what each might see or feel.

One third-floor room Bevy entered had no furnishings but a large, free-standing mirror, framed in ornately carved wood, a standard bedroom fixture of the 1800s. Before this particular mirror stood a dark-haired man studying his reflection and muttering softly.

He did not return Bevy's nod of greeting or even look at her, and she assumed he was a tenant or a workman who had stopped at the mirror to check his appearance. His nondescript clothing suggested nothing other-worldly. Bevy's whole impression was of a living person and she passed by him to look out a dirty window. The cluttered area below had obviously once been a formal flower garden, and she felt sad that such a fine property had been abandoned to ruin. Bevy was also disappointed that she would have little to report when the group reassembled.

For part of her time in the room, Bevy had been aware of the man's voice continuing its mutter, but when she turned her attention from the cheerless scene below, he was gone. She walked close enough to the mirror to touch its smooth wood and joined Ray, who waited for her in the hall. While she answered her husband's questions about whether anything had happened, Bevy turned toward the room and saw that the strange man was back, in exactly the position she'd first seen him. He vanished before she could tell Ray to look.

"At that point," Bevy says, "I knew why the back of my neck felt tingly and why my feet were suddenly icy cold. I had just walked through a ghost!"

Creepy Enough?

A number of *Missouri Ghosts* readers expressed disappointment that so few of that book's stories were really scary. This one should satisfy them:

In October of 1937, the *Washington University Medical Alumni Quarterly* recounted an experience of Joseph Nash McDowell, an anatomist who lived from 1805 to 1868 and became prominent in the state's medical history. His was the era before Missouri law allowed medical schools legal access to human cadavers for instructional and experimental work. Individuals who were called "resurrectionists" or "body-snatchers" provided these for a high fee. McDowell was not the only teacher who sometimes took students to the graveyard to secure bodies on their own. However, because he was a spiritualist, such activity caused him a great deal of guilt and fear.

In this case, McDowell knew of a young German girl who had died of an unusual disease, one he felt should be studied. He led a party to exhume her, but news of their action leaked out. McDowell was warned by friends that the girl's outraged family members would soon be at the school with demands for her body and for reparation against all who had a part in disturbing her grave.

McDowell went to the college at eleven o'clock that night to hide the girl's body. His destination was the attic, where some unusual arrangement in the rafters would allow concealment. As recounted in the alumni publication:

"I had ascended one flight of stairs when out went my lamp. I laid down the corpse and re-struck a light. I then picked up the body, when out went my light again. I felt for another match in my pocket, when I distinctly saw my dear, old mother who had been dead these many years, standing a little distance off, beckoning to me. In the middle of the passage was a window; I saw her in front of it. I walked along close to the wall with the corpse over my shoulder and went to the top loft and hid it."

Being very familiar with his surroundings, McDowell descended in the dark, which enabled him to look down the stairwell without being seen and watch three armed men starting up from the ground floor. McDowell's only possible hiding place was the dissection room, which he knew would be their first stop. Looking in, he saw "my spirit mother standing near the table from which I had just taken the corpse." The halo surrounding his mother helped McDowell see the table clearly and take the unfortunate girl's place, pulling over his face the sheet that had covered hers.

McDowell does not describe the fear and stress he felt, sharing a corpse's sheet, aware that his career and the school's reputation were at risk, not to mention his own life. He says only, "I lay like marble."

The party of men entered and began lifting sheets. McDowell knew that the first two bodies were male, the next two dark haired women; the German maiden had blonde hair. At McDowell's table one man commented, "Here's a fellow who died in his boots" and did not bother to lift the sheet. McDowell wrote of an inexplicable urge to raise up and frighten the searchers, but his mother whispered to him, "Be still."

McDowell continued to lie like marble, listening as the men visited every room in the building. When they finally left, he was able to slip out without being noticed. Next day the danger seemed to have blown over and he wrote, "We dissected the body, buried the fragments and had no further trouble." He does not remark on whether or not the terrifying episode yielded anything of scientific value. McDowell became one of the state's leading surgeons and a founder of the first successful medical college west of the Mississippi.

A Much-Viewed Ghost

"Why do people keep moving out of that house?"
"There's something...."
Jim Riek, news anchor for television station NBC8 in Columbia, says those words have been exchanged many times about his childhood home in Jefferson City. Several people who have lived in the 150-year-old house reported seeing the apparition of a young girl there. Some spoke freely of it on a televised news feature with Riek in May of 1999.

Fred Seaman, former councilman for Jefferson City, bought the house in 1973. Though nothing harmed or even frightened anyone, the family found definitely unusual aspects to their new home. One sunshiny day Seaman awoke from a nap, aware of movement in the room. He looked up and saw a little girl walking away from him down the hallway. She turned, glanced back and went into the bathroom. He followed her and found the room empty. Seaman says the child was wearing a long white dress or perhaps a nightgown, and had something in her hair, a ribbon or flower.

Seaman's daughter became accustomed to footsteps on the stairs near her own bedroom door. After looking in vain for the cause, she accepted the sounds as just another quirk of the house. "Living there made Halloween kind of special," Seaman laughs.

Riek himself, as a child, sometimes saw the ghost's dress hem in his peripheral vision as he played on the floor. In these earliest instances he would feel someone approaching and then pausing beside him, as any child might to watch another's play. If he looked up, hoping to see all of her, there usually was nothing, but by looking down, he could see her again, from the corner of his eye.

Today Riek comments that he saw this little ghost hundreds of times during his 18 years in the house, and that she looked as substantial and real as any living person. Sometimes he saw her more than once in a day. Sometimes he did not see her for a month at a time. Riek says he occasionally saw enough of the little ghost to know that her garment was ivory or cream-colored, and rather formal looking, with a high neck and buttons up the front. It covered her feet completely; he could not see whether or not she wore shoes.

One of Riek's big regrets is that he never questioned his late mother more about the story of the house. He remembers that she didn't believe at first the local tale that a little girl had died a terrible death there. Supposedly, the child fell into a pig sty and was killed by the animals. Mrs. Riek researched the matter enough to be convinced that such a death did occur, but Jim does not remember her ever discussing it in full. Somehow the family did not talk about the ghost much, did not share details of their experiences with it.

One of the residents of the house after the Rieks left it hired someone to come there and search with a metal detector for something unrelated to the stories. Riek says that in the area where the pig pen had been, they discovered a tiny plain gold band of the type fashionable for children in the early 1900s and before.

One incident in history of the place might be interpreted as a benevolent act from the little ghost: Harold Krieger, a Jefferson City accountant, 50 years ago, as a child playing hide and seek with friends, found an old gas refrigerator in the basement and he got into it.

Young Krieger was horrified to find that he could not get out and he knew that his mother was shopping and would be away for hours. He did not become the second child to die on the property, however. By some means, there in the dark, he found the very small hole through which gas had been piped into the box. He breathed through that opening until he was missed and rescued.

Riek's television program about his childhood home included comments from some professors of psychology. One of these, Frank Cleary, from St. Louis University, said scientific research still has not produced proof against many of para psychology's contentions. He said "We live in a mysterious world and nobody knows everything." Dr. James Houran, of Southern Illinois University, concurred: "...we cannot dismiss things just because we don't understand them; many of these matters need to be taken seriously."

*"Sweet haunt, I hear the
clatter of your chains,
Whose links make song,
whose strength detains...."*
actor James Cagney

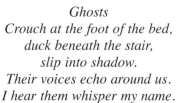

Ghosts
Crouch at the foot of the bed,
duck beneath the stair,
slip into shadow.
Their voices echo around us.
I hear them whisper my name.
Elizabeth Hanley.

Chapter Two

More
Apparitions

"Ask me not," he said, and moving
Passed into the distance dim.
High the sun stood in the heavens,
But no shadow followed him.
Stevie Smith's poem, *The Parklands*

Iron County gives us a nice, long story in the old tradition of both romance and gross details. It's said to have taken place in 1860, during an era when Missouri's Methodist Churches sponsored a small college at Arcadia. Many such schools existed at the time, offering young people higher education without the expenses and other problems of traveling far from home. Some were able to commute to these schools each day, but probably more stayed on campus or boarded in the town.

Near Arcadia lived Judge Allen Hollomon with his wife and their large family of children, a few of whom attended the nearby college. Hollomon was one of the most prominent men in the area, owner of a mill and a great deal of land that included several rental farms. Possibly to help them control activities of their own children, the Hollomons made their home more or less an open house for young people. Students gathered there on weekend nights for visiting, games, music and refreshments. The walk from the campus was not long and overarching trees made it picturesque and pleasant in almost any weather.

Among Hollomon's numerous descendants was a grandson named Paul Hinchey, born the year after events that created a family ghost story with such distasteful aspects that it was spoken of in whispers, if at all, while he grew up. In maturity Hinchey wrote down all he had been able to find out, carefully giving fictitious names to the real people whose lives had been affected.

The students coming to Hollomons' frequently included a young woman beautiful in appearance, personality and character, whom Hinchey called Agnes Powell. Though she was popular, Agnes never paired up with any young man for outings, and declined invitations for anything but group activities. She seemed to be taking care not to show particular interest in any one suitor.

The exception was a boy Hinchey called Doug Miller. Doug came from far enough back in the Ozark hills that his speech and manners were different from his classmates' and he was very anxious to change this. Handsome and a good student, he wanted to make the social impression necessary to realize his ambitions. Perhaps Doug appealed to Agnes for help; perhaps she volunteered it, but she did devote many hours to tutoring Doug on diction and etiquette. She was always careful, however, that the two of them were never alone together.

One afternoon when Doug happened to be absent, the mystery of Agnes' aloofness was solved. An expensive carriage drawn by a fine team of bays pulled up to the judge's gate and at sight of the young man alighting, Agnes ran and clasped him in warm embrace.

"My fiance!" she told her friends proudly, and then the couple explained how they had been secretly plighted for years. Robert Baker had waited to declare himself to his beloved's father until he could truthfully say he had the wherewithal to keep Agnes in the comfort she'd always known. The father now had given his blessing, and Baker wanted Agnes to leave with him the following morning for their home town and begin wedding preparations.

Agnes' friends were sorry to lose her sweet company but rejoiced with her. They were still twittering about the perfection of it all when Doug Miller joined them on the evening of the day Agnes departed. He became silent, his face held carefully blank, so all his schoolmates realized with pity that he had read too much into Agnes' attention to him. Nobody knew what to do or say as Doug broke away and abruptly hurried off.

Doug was not in classes for the next few days, but nobody sought him out; his friends supposed he preferred not facing them just yet. When they found he'd abandoned his rental room, they assumed he was so hurt and humiliated he had gone back home. In their conversation, though, they discovered that nobody really knew exactly where he was from. Some were sure he'd said both his parents were dead and that he'd sold his legacy, the family farm, to finance his education. He had nowhere to go, so where was he?

Before long, young people strolling the road to Hollomons' began remarking on an unpleasant odor, and the misfortune that must have befallen some wild animal or domestic beast. As days passed, the odor grew so strong that attendance at the gatherings fell off.

A couple of the young men, perhaps suspecting the truth, followed the smell to its source and were aghast to find that someone had hanged himself in the woods. The body's clothing and a nearby hat told them it was Doug Miller.

They immediately sought Judge Hollomon's advice and his first word to them was to tell nobody for the time

being. He summoned the sheriff and after consultation these two community leaders told the boys to bring digging tools from Holloman's barn. All four went together to deal with Doug's body. The judge and sheriff decreed that for health reasons Doug must be buried at once. They directed digging right under his hanging body so it would fall into the grave when cut down. The condition of the body and embalming methods of the time left little choice, particularly since nobody had any idea who, if anyone, would want to know about Doug's death. Though this seems callous by today's standards, we must remember that options were limited in that era.

All involved were much distressed that a good, hopeful, hard-working young person must die wretchedly and be buried like an animal grown offensive, buried with no marker. They swore to each other to keep the secret, but it got out and other secrets led to others and others.

First strange report came from the judge's two youngest sons. Within a week or so of the burial, they said they were awakened by the watch dog's barking and saw, in moonlight streaming through their second-story window, a young man sitting on the sill. When the brothers advanced toward the image it disappeared, but they had looked long enough to be agreed that it was Doug Miller. Down in the yard, they could see their dog staring, rapt, in the direction of the woods where Miller had hanged himself.

Their father ordered the boys not to talk about this outside the family, but other people began to report seeing an unknown man walking in the tunnel of trees that led to Hollomon's. Even more dramatic, one of the older Hollomon sons, riding home from town one night, had unaccustomed trouble with his normally docile horse. It balked and could not be made to take another step into the tunnel. After trying everything that a horse-savvy young man of the day knew to try, he gave up and rode back to town. There he waited until he found two horsemen together who would be passing his father's house. By positioning his mount between theirs, he was able to get home.

After a few weeks, strange happenings in the tunnel abated and gradually the tragedy lost its priority in conversation. Students could once more concentrate on school and gatherings at the judge's, which had become almost as big and jolly as ever.

But in a year or so a traveler through town asked whether Doug Miller was still in the college and explained his curiosity: the couple who bought the house where Doug was reared had been asking about him. Someone who looked like Doug was moving around their property. This person appeared by night and by day and acted strangely. They were becoming fearful. Where was Doug? Was he sure enough still alive and in school?

Connoisseurs of things ghostly would say this is a classic example of a spirit leaving its body under conditions of such mental anguish that some time was needed for gaining strength to face the next stage of existence. They would say it was perfectly natural for Doug Miller's spirit to stay near the scene of his death for a few weeks. He had finally gained enough orientation to get back home and from there, if all went as it should, he would soon strike off into the hereafter. Paul Hinchey did not remark about the length of time Doug may have been said to haunt his early environment. He did comment in his paper that Agnes and her husband were never bothered by the sad ghost of a young man who had loved her too much.

A Phantom With a Purpose

Perhaps there should be a chapter just about ghosts who seem to have a reason for appearing, or for ghosts who—despite what the experts tell us—seem to have physical power. Such a one appeared in a paper connected with Mark Twain that may or may not be totally fiction. The famous writer at times declared himself a skeptic about the supernatural, yet it's on record that from 1885 to 1903 he was a member of the American Society for Psychical Research. What follows appeared in the Autumn, 1948, issue of *The Pacific Spectator.*

The article, titled "Ghost Life on the Mississippi," was introduced by a supposed great niece who said the manuscript turned up in her childhood home where Clemens was a frequent visitor. She also said that the famous writer's mother was a great believer in ghosts and had a large collection of accounts of supernatural experiences that were personal or came from people she knew.

The story that followed concerned a riverboat pilot named William Jones. On a certain wildly stormy night, he defied his captain, who told him to tie the boat up because they were nearing an especially dangerous bend in the river and driving snow would make it too hard for him to navigate. Having earlier that day been derided by some of his colleagues for his pomposity and called "King of Pilots," Jones was in a mood for showing everyone a thing or two. He safely took the boat, *Boreas,* through snag-infested shallows with sharp bends that were challenging on a clear day. To another pilot who tried to discourage him, he was said to reply, "I'll take her through if the devil seizes me for it five minutes afterward."

Jones was never seen again, though some blood stains on the deck indicated someone had been injured there. When the *Boreas* reached St. Louis, she was sold, laid up for refurbishment and not taken out again for almost a year. When she went, one of her pilots was a man called Joseph Millard, who had known Jones and his great feat. Millard was resolved to never do anything so foolhardy. When weather signs pointed to a bad night, he began at once to look for a safe place to tie up. Unfortunately, hard-driven snow descended on the boat before he reached refuge, and because he could not see the bank, Millard had the engines turned off.

Gradually, alone there in the dark, Millard began to feel a strange presence, and soon, by occasional flashes of light that came from holes in the stovepipe, he saw a vaguely outlined human form opposite him at the wheel. One larger than usual flash revealed the terrible, ravaged face of William Jones. "Fixed and lusterless eyes," Clemens wrote, and he described disheveled hair and bloated appearance suggesting a drowned corpse.

According to the story, Millard's "blood curdled in his veins and he trembled in every limb." He could neither move nor speak and could not prevent the wheel's being wrenched from him. The signal to restart engines was given and as power returned, Millard watched the wheel make calm and delicate movements as if in a master hand. He expected momentary crashing sounds, but none came. Flashes of light showed Millard's guest turned toward the door, then opening it and departing.

"You've outdone Jones himself," Millard's relief pilot told him in awe a few minutes later. Conclusion of this story and no doubt proof that it is fiction, was that the two men found on the floor a pocket watch, crystal broken, but engraved with Jones' name. If there is any truth to this, it may be that an angry pilot once did an amazing feat to silence his critics. But Dorothy Shrader of Hermann, daughter and granddaughter of riverboat men, confirms that in earlier years the sincere belief in ghosts was deeper and more common than it is today. In *Steamboat Treasures*, second volume in her trilogy of river books, she told how easily roustabouts and deck hands could be kept at their work long after hours. They merely had to be reminded that after midnight, ghosts could walk. Everyone had best finish loading or unloading while they could do so safely!

From a Reliable Source

For many years the late Leonard Hall of Caledonia wrote a highly respected column for *The St. Louis Globe Democrat* and when that newspaper folded, for *The St. Louis Post Dispatch*. I never saw him deal with any subjects but nature, rural living and conservation. However, a friend tells me that Hall did a column in his later years, describing an event he had discussed with nobody until that time.

It took place on a sandbar in the upper Current, while Hall was on a float trip with several other people. Wakened by unfamiliar sounds, he left his cot to look out the tent door. Not more than 100 yards away, he said, were campfires attended by Indians in breech clouts. Around the fires, eating, sat men wearing armor which he recognized as Spanish by the helmet style. The sight was so stunning and bizarre that Hall just went back to bed, thinking he was dreaming or hallucinating and embarrassed to call anyone else to look. But the minutely detailed incident stayed vividly in mind. If he was going to hallucinate, why about Spanish soldiers?

Although the friend did not say so, Hall might well have questioned the good sense of men wearing their armor to dinner. Surely the first thing they wanted, at the end of the day, was to be rid of it. It would be hot in summer, cold in cold weather, and would severely limit movement. Some types of armor would have made it difficult to sit down on the ground and maybe impossible to get up without help. On the other hand, if they did not fully trust their guides, or if they feared being picked off by arrows shot from the dark, maybe soldiers would leave on helmets and whatever protected their backs and chests, at least until cooking fires were out and the diners were less obvious targets.

In any case, many years later Hall came across the fact that Hernando DeSoto led a party into the area in 1561 and that they used Indian guides. Possibly experts would classify what Hall saw not as apparitions, but as an example of time slip, of people inexplicably drifting for a few minutes into someone else's time.

Now You See It

Another type of apparition discussed often in archives of the supernatural casts its images onto film, though the photographer sees no one before him. In 1984, a *Missouri Life* article about Missouri ghosts told of a man in Iron County who went to visit the farm where he grew up. The place had changed hands and the house had been extensively remodeled. From outside, however, one portion looked much the same as in his childhood and he decided to take a picture of the low-roofed back porch where he often played.

When his film was developed, one of the windows seemed to hold a fairly distinct image of a man with a white beard, apparently leaning close to the panes from a sitting position. It resembled an elderly family member, long deceased, who had in his last years of life spent most of his time sitting by that window, in that position.

The visitor, having been inside the house, knew that base cabinets had been built under the windows of that particular room. There was no way a person could have been sitting there, so as a test, the photographer showed the picture, without comment, to several of his siblings and cousins. Some of them exclaimed involuntarily, "Look! That looks like....!" Others saw nothing, which is why collecting ghost stories is so fascinating.

"Jeremy?" "Sweetheart?" "What do you fear?"
"Nothing, my darling. Nothing is here."
"Jeremy?" "Sweetheart?" "What do you you flee?"
"Something...I don't know...Something I see."

William Rose Benet,
The Skater on Ghost Lake

Then shall the dust return to the earth as it was: and the spirit shall return unto God who gave it.
The Bible, Ecclesiastes

the Lord. . . In whose hand is the soul of every living thing.
Job 12, 9-10,
King James Version of the Bible

Who knows whether the spirit of a human being goes upward or whether the spirit of a beast goes downward to the earth?
Ecclesiastes, The Revised English Bible

But man dieth and wasteth away; yea, man giveth up the ghost, and where is he?
The Bible, Job

He was eaten of worms and gave up the ghost.
The Bible, Acts

Chapter Three

Still More Apparitions

*I'm sure they're there, but if I met one, I'd not be
as scared as I am of the nuts I meet every day.*
Harry Truman when asked about White House ghosts

If you want to get rid of a ghost, take a couple of
dashes through it. It will disappear. At least this is possible according to the *Washington County Journal* for
April 25, 1867. Marie Edgar of Potosi kindly photo-
copied two lengthy stories for me from this publication.
The *Journal* does not explain whether the stories are
fiction or originally related by somebody as fact. They
are done in a tradition of writing that seems to us unbear-
ably redundant in conversation and detail, but we must
admit that these writers knew how to create atmosphere.
A taste:

"What quaint weird stories about ghosts or spirits
come across one every now and then, at the most unlikely times, stories so utterly dissimilar that it is quite
impossible to generalize from them.

"Sometimes the ghost is seen in the conventional
white sheet; more often it does not appear at all, but is
only heard. A ghostly footfall echoes on the stairs; a
wailing cry outside the window rouses the sleeper; some-

times only part of a form appears, as when, in one well known family, a ghastly head, white, wet, dripping with blood, is seen or said to be seen, before a death. At other times, as in the last ghost story I heard, which I am about to write down, the ghost sticks pertinaciously to the same room in the same dress and mutters the same words."

The narrator then relays a friend's experience while visiting at Grasgarth Hall in North Yorkshire, England. Chatting one summer evening "just before the candles were brought in," the friend learned of an aristocratic family that formerly owned the place. By 1745, a year of rebellion, only two survivors remained, twin brothers. These were James, the younger, and Sir Hugh, older by only half an hour.

When the undescribed unrest began, a prince wrote requesting the brothers' help, asking them to bring every man they could muster. Sir Hugh excitedly began planning an immediate departure with all their able-bodied male servants. James was alarmed at what this could do to the operation of their farm and objected passionately. He argued that it was foolish to risk livelihood and lives just for the sake of a prince's conception of his honor. The result was a bitter quarrel, made even worse by the fact that both brothers were drinking heavily.

Servants who had been eavesdropping were relieved when the two reeled off upstairs to their beds. But next day, neither of the men could be roused for breakfast. About midday, having found James' room empty, the servants broke into Sir Hugh's room and discovered him dead, his head in a pool of blood they assumed had come from falling or being thrown against the bloodied marble fireplace mantel. James was crouched in a chair, eyes vacant, muttering over and over "I didn't do it! I didn't do it!" The story was that James never regained his senses and that Hugh's spirit walked uneasily.

The guest said this story did not trouble his sleeping in the least that night. But on a subsequent visit he was assigned a different room, one with a massive, elaborate marble chimney piece incorporating the mantel. About an hour after falling asleep, he awoke with a start, as if someone had spoken to him.

Sitting in the chair by the fireplace was a man "...with face white and ghastly." The personage wore a full wig with long formal curls, and a sudden flare-up of the flickering, dying fire, showed an embroidered vest clearly, with long-flapped waistcoat and knee breeches. The figure's lips moved continuously.

For what seemed several minutes, the apparition stayed in this guise and it must have looked like a living person, despite the antique clothing and wig, because the guest asked him who he was and why he was there. The fire's light temporarily disappeared altogether, as is typical when fires are dying. Its next flare-up showed the man standing, staring into the flame, lips still moving.

"I then thought I could see through the figure," the guest had told his friend, "but not distinctly, for he was between me and the seat of the chair and while I could just see its back plainly, the rest was obscured as by a fog."

Gathering all his courage, the guest rose from his bed and walked to the figure, which took no notice of him, but kept looking into the fire, now audibly muttering, "I didn't do it. I didn't do it."

So here, before 1876, we have another walk-through portrayed, though it might more accurately be called a run-through, for the guest charged on the image as if to attack. The effect he described, was "...a fog seemed to hang round and a clammy chill made my skin creep, while a faint, sickly taste and smell made me throw myself almost fainting into the chair and close my eyes."

When he finally looked again, the figure was gone, leaving behind a thin white smoky substance. But as the guest watched, this slowly compacted back into the shape of a man. Incredibly, the guest charged it again, and this time — though he once more had the sickening taste and other sensations — the figure did not return.

The guest apparently did not explain to his friend why he felt compelled to attack the figure a second time. He says only that he pulled the coverings over his head and remained so until daylight, certain from time to time that he heard the monotonous murmur "I didn't do it."

He ended his story with typical British understatement: "You may imagine that I never slept in that room again."

Another Ghost With a Goal

Unfulfilled desire or determination to complete some important task are supposedly the reasons for many ghostly manifestations, but these do not appear conclusively very often. The other *Washington County Journal* photocopy supplied by Marie Edgar contains a touching example of a ghost with a goal. This story appeared in November of 1870 and was presented as a true account written by a doctor whose practice began in 1843. The incident came the following year.

Being at that time eager for any patients he could get, the doctor had set up a bell that could be rung from the street if someone needed emergency help. For three straight nights he was awakened by the bell's ringing, but, he said, in a timid, tentative way. Each time he dressed and rushed down only to find nobody in the street or anywhere in sight. Intent on solving the mystery, the doctor stayed up the next night and stationed himself near the door, so he could open it before the bell ringer escaped.

His plan worked and what he found was a little girl of maybe nine years, barefooted, though it was winter, dressed only in petticoats, clutching a piece of blanket around her body instead of a coat. Rather than feeling wrath, the doctor was of course overcome with pity and concern. He asked the child what she needed. "Mama is dying. Come quick, Sir," the child said, her lips moving slowly, as with great effort. She admitted having been at his bell before. As she led him through the streets, he was able to find out that her name was Susy, but she would say nothing else. She led him to just the kind of trashy alleys he expected, and up three flights in a slum house to the unheated garret. There he found a woman beyond his help, delirious and barely alive. The child having disappeared once he was in the attic, the doctor asked where she was, realizing she needed to be taken to refuge.

"She's over yonder," the mother managed to whisper, "starved I guess, been dead these three days." Taking the failing candle the doctor walked across the room to what appeared to be only a pile of bedding. There, as anyone who's ever read a ghost story could predict, was little Susy. Though obviously not newly dead, the doctor had no doubt she was the same little wanderer who exerted herself bravely to try to help her mother. A notation at the end of this story said it had first appeared in *Lippincott's Magazine*. Nothing indicated whether it was acknowledged fiction or, perhaps, based on fact.

A Contrite Mother

A shorter and more modern purposeful ghost was described in one of Jim Longo's books, *Ghosts Along the Mississippi*. This was a conventional ghost: white, indefinable, related to the history of a house. She — for the first person to see her was certain of the femininity —

first appeared when the resident family's children were ill. It was not a life-threatening situation, but very stressful for the mother, because more than one child was sick at once and she had to attend them day and night. She first met the entity in a hallway and was terrified. Later, when she found the thing sitting on the edge of a child's bed, she was aware of something weary and loving in its posture.

As happens so often, the woman's husband was skeptical of her account, rather understandably since she said the entity had neither arms nor legs, that she could see, but she was certain it was a woman. He said that an anxious mother, short of sleep, could easily hallucinate.

But then their daughter, unaware of her mother's experience, reported one very similar. At that point, the father began researching the house to see what might have happened there that would cause haunting.

He learned that among former tenants had been another couple with a few young children. The father of that family, however, developed heart problems and could barely summon strength to maintain family income through his job. The yard and house exterior soon began to look neglected, and his wife fretted. At times she urged him to do just a little outside work. When he finally did undertake some repairs, he collapsed and died.

The wife was, of course, distraught, feeling that she had robbed her children of their father. Obsessing threw her into a depression that ended with her killing herself in the bathtub. This is a classic example of one theory about ghosts; afterlife realization of the consequences of actions can cause guilt so deep that a spirit finds rest impossible.

The modern-day father's findings confirmed his own family's certainty that their ghost was benevolent. As time passed, they all adjusted to her presence and the mother confessed to making a kind of companion of the spirit. She talked aloud to it about the kinds of things she liked to discuss with her living women friends. Though she sensed a pleasant response to her conversation, the mother said their ghost's greatest activity came during illness or other stressful times. It seemed understandable that she was trying to make up for abdicating her responsibilities.

We might find it more logical if this motherly spirit had ministered to her own children, wherever they were as they grew up, and to their children, wherever they were. But maybe she did. Maybe a ghost can be in more than one place at a time or can easily go from one place to another as needed. What to we really know for sure about ghosts?

(Author's note: Jim Longo is a college professor who writes about many other things than ghosts — Brazil and the history of the Shakers, for instance. He is working on a new ghost book, to be available, as his other ghost books are, from White Chapel Publications, 1-888-Ghostly, and from Borders and other book stores.)

Ward's Fog

Another apparition variation comes from Frank Ward's book, *Close Behind Thee*, published in 1998 (available from White Chapel Publications) and he presents it as happening to him in Ozark County. The year was 1941 with World War II in progress. Ward was a serviceman who had been visiting his parents in West Plains but wanted also to see his grandparents in Decateur, IL before his leave was up, because he was going overseas. He had no way to travel but by hitch-hiking, safer then than now.

When one of his rides ended at a rural crossroads, Ward began walking and describes it as not too unpleasant. Though the night air was chilly, a fairly bright moon enabled him to see well enough. Edges of the road were a bit gloomy because he was in fringes of the Mark Twain Forest and trees came close in on both sides.

After an hour or so of walking, Ward sat down at the side of the road to rest, apparently not dismayed that he could see no town or farm lights, and that only a couple of cars had passed since he began. The peaceful view ahead of him included a dip in the road, where fog began to gather, "...like a silvery blanket..." he said.

Then, to Ward's alarm, the scene became decidedly eerie. The fog swirled into a column about eight feet high and gradually took on the shape of a man. This was only about twenty feet away, and as Ward watched, the strange formation turned toward him. He describes breaking into a cold sweat and being ready to flee. The image, however, melted back into fog and disappeared.

Understandably reluctant to walk into what he had just witnessed, Ward turned back in the direction he had come, telling himself he'd walk all the way home to West Plains before he'd go into the remnants of fog remaining in that frightful low place.

Fortunately for him a bus came by and though he had no money for fare, Ward was able to catch onto the ladder and cling there until the bus stopped in a town where he jumped off unnoticed. "I thought I would freeze to death," he commented about the time he spent in the vehicle's slipstream. But anything was better than walking into fog that he knew could shape itself into...something else. A note about the bus ladder: at that time luggage was stored on top of buses, reached by a metal ladder that curved over the end of the vehicle and onto the roof.

This story is one of the few we have with an outdoor setting on an atmospheric night and brings to mind this quotation from August Derleth's story "The Lonesome Place".

"You who sit in your houses of nights, you who sit in the theaters, you who are gay at dances and parties — all of you who are enclosed by four walls — you have no conception of what goes on outside in the dark, in the lonesome places."

We will come back, come back again
As long as the red earth rolls.
He never wasted a leaf or a tree.
Do you think he would squander souls?

Rudyard Kipling

"I'll be around — and around and
around and around and around...."
from the song *The Highwayman*
by Kris Kristofferson and sung on a
recording of the same name with
Willie Nelson, Waylon Jennings and
Johnny Cash.

I believe I shall, in some shape or
other, always exist; and, with all the
inconveniences human life is liable
to, I shall not object to a new edition
of mine, hoping, however, that the
errata of the last may be corrected.

Benjamin Franklin

Chapter Four

Poltergeists

They are not really spirits or ghosts in the true sense of the word. Poltergeists are random energy psychokinetically generated by a living person.

Chris Woodyard on web site, invink.com

Among its "rackety ghost" manifestations, Missouri seems to have had one who was overgenerous with water and another who drew pictures. Both were responsive to reprimands which seems to be fairly typical of the beings Germans named with a word meaning, approximately, "noisy spirit" or "mischievous, playful ghost." The doings of these entities usually seem pointless and silly, like the antics of many young boys. Households afflicted by poltergeists, say the investigators, usually contain a troubled teenager or two. What adolescent is not at times frustrated with parental restraints and angry at the whole world? We're told that these intense emotions somehow cause objects to move about, or they can create strange sounds and smells. Many poltergeist cases have been resolved when young people were caught in the act of deliberately staging odd occurrences, even setting fires.

Occasionally poltergeist activity seems to start simply and become complex and dangerous. Such a progression was recorded in the book, *Possession*, a non-fiction account of events that formed the basis for the novel and the movie both called *The Exorcist*. Some poltergeists seem to be minor facets of a haunting that has other mysterious activity. For instance, the Lemp Mansion in St. Louis has poltergeist activity in addition to reports of at least one apparition, and a number of puzzling sounds and sensations. Some of the most common dilemmas in the Lemp House, now that it's a popular restaurant and a bed and breakfast, are non-threatening and at times amusing. Objects sometimes seem to move about under their own power, or to disappear, only to turn up later in unlikely places. This is routine poltergeist stuff, but no teenagers have inhabited the Lemp Mansion on a daily basis throughout its latest segment of history.

Poltergeists are perhaps the hardest of all entities to categorize. Our stories about them are widely varied, and an expert in ghostliness might say most of these are not true poltergeists.

A Haunted Church

Nobody connected with this story was willing to be quoted, but several have reported perplexing events in a small county church built in the 1930s after a tornado destroyed its predecessor.

The minister says that on Saturdays, alone in the building, working on the church bulletin, he has become accustomed to a game of musical doors. He must move through several areas of the church to complete the steps of printing the weekly bulletin and then distributing it to the place where ushers expect to find it, with one copy going to his pulpit. Frequently he has found that doors he closed stood wide open when he next passed them, and others he had just opened were closed tight.

The church organist, alone to practice, has more than once made a hurried exit because of overwhelming feelings of danger, almost as if a voice were saying urgently,

"You must get out of here! Come on! Get out while you can!" Could this be a ghostly prank, or perhaps remnants of emotion left over from the day of the tornado?

The custodian says work equipment often seems lost but then appears in surprising places. He's never surprised to find Sunday School supplies dumped on the classroom floors.

Once during an area-wide gathering of women's missionary groups, a visitor approached the minister and asked him, "What's going on here? All day I've been seeing movements at the edge of my vision, but when I turn and try to see clearly, there's nothing. This is really spooky. What is it?"

What are we to make of such things, especially since poltergeist-like actions sometimes seem designed to give comfort? Sue Webster of Columbia says that about 18 years ago when she and her husband were starting to Indiana for her father's funeral, their garage door gently lowered of its own accord. Neither of them had activated it and their home was not located where someone else's device could have done so. This had never happened before and it has not happened since, except for one more time about sixteen years ago, when Sue's husband died. Did his spirit remember that Sue had greeted the first event with gratitude, saying "Oh, that's Dad, letting us know he's okay and still with us!

Put It In Writing, Please

Paul Pepper, a well-known and much-beloved television personality in Columbia, speaks matter of factly about the spirits that in his house were lavish with water, possibly aimed poorly at his plants while he was away on vacation. Pepper felt he had his house plants set up ideally for survival during his absence, but had arranged

for a neighbor to check in on them. He was dismayed, returning home, to find his sink running over with water and a great deal of damage done to carpets.

Pepper knew he had not left the water running and could not imagine that vandals would have stopped with only one destructive act. None of his belongings were harmed or missing. The neighbor said she had not turned on any faucet. She watered nothing; nothing needed it. All friends who had keys to Paul's house were above suspicion; none would consider it funny to damage someone's home.

Next time he went on vacation, Pepper left this note on the kitchen counter: "Dear Poltergeists: Have a good time, but please don't do anything destructive. Thank you, Paul." All his trips since then have included tranquil homecomings.

Do I Make Myself Clear?

Another Missourian stopped a poltergeist with her righteous indignation, sharply expressed.

She is Melinda Reisenleiter of Hallsville. When she and Keith Hawkins moved into one of the oldest houses in town, one that had been surrounded by farm land when it was built, a few friends warned of its reputation for being haunted. Then a workman told them, "There's something here...." A friend who had come while the couple was gone told them, "I sat down to wait for you, but got a strong feeling that I wasn't alone — and that I wasn't welcome!"

The spirit never manifested to the house's human residents in any alarming way, but things moved around a lot. For instance, Keith describes a cup and saucer from a collection housed on an open shelf: one cup and one saucer appeared in the middle of the floor, cup neatly in saucer, both unchipped. "This would have been impossible if some shock or vibration caused them to fly off the shelf," he said.

In the old Hallsville house the couple heard inexplicable, aimless sounds, one being like soft rope slashing against an upstairs window pane, yet no tree branches were within reach of the window. Small hand prints appeared on freshly washed windows, even as the couple worked. Melinda sometimes felt a tug on her shirt tail, the kind a demanding child might make to get attention.

The two searched their property's abstract and the memory of Hallsville elders, looking for clues as to what ghost-making event might have taken place in their house. They found nothing. Nobody knew of a child who had died there suddenly or tragically. Melinda and Keith grew accustomed to their playful guest — whom they felt sure was a young boy — and even became rather fond of him. But then something more remarkable happened.

Before the couple moved in, all the walls had been freshly painted, including those inside closets. They'd packed one closet tightly with movers' boxes that could wait indefinitely to be opened. The closet was so full that nobody could possibly have squeezed to the back wall and found space there to do art work. Yet when the last box was finally taken out, there on the wall was a simple, childlike drawing of a rabbit.

This seemed to refer to Melinda's scolding the poltergeist and giving him an ultimatum about teasing their pet rabbit. They had enjoyed the animal for several years. Litter trained, the rabbit had free run of the house and had always been a cheerful and confident pet. Gradually, in their new home, she grew hyper-alert and nervous, often thumping her feet in panic. Her appetite declined and she was usually hiding when they returned from work. To the couple this seemed like behavior that would only result from relentless teasing. Melinda could not stand the thought of their helpless and innocent little pet being confined all day with an inescapable tormentor.

"So I went through all the rooms of the house," she says, "talking out loud, telling our guest that he was welcome to stay with us as long as he wanted, if he stopped teasing the rabbit. If he didn't stop, I told him, we'd get whatever help we needed to throw him out."

Slowly the rabbit regained most of her former disposition. Then, as months and years passed, the poltergeist could have been growing up and developing new interests. He did not seem to be around as much and what he did was less troublesome. Now, unusual activity in the house has almost completely stopped. Melinda and Keith miss it and so do their guests.

The Case Of The Homing Gloves

One Missourian who asked for anonymity had an unforgettable experience one holiday season with some gift gloves. It was 1966 and he was recently bereaved of his father. The year before, the man whom we'll call Carl had been touched and pleased with a handsome pair of gloves his parents gave him. These seemed a precious link with his father and he was careful to preserve them.

When he went home for the family's first Christmas without his father, Carl and his sister were delegated to get a tree from a nearby lot. He decided to take his gloves off, even though it was cold. "I'd had some experience of what cedar sap can do to leather," he says. "I remarked on this to my sister and she saw me throw the gloves into the front seat." The siblings got their tree and took it home and the evening was devoted to quiet festivity.

Next day, Carl started to drive somewhere and needed his gloves. To his great surprise, they were not in the car. He searched the driveway and the house, then drove back to the Christmas tree lot to see if his gloves had fallen out there, and perhaps been turned in. Back at his mother's house, he looked again in the hall, and every possible place he could have dropped the gloves. "I'm not an absent minded person," Carl says. "I'm not someone who can't keep track of the small details of life." The rest of his visit was saddened by the fact that he had lost something cherished as a reminder of his father. He felt very guilty for letting this happen.

But back at his own house, Carl's first move was to take off his overcoat and hang in the hall closet. There, on the shelf where he always put his hats and gloves, were the missing pair. "What explanation could there be?" he asks. "My mother and my sister both knew that I drove down there wearing those gloves. I felt just like I had when I was a child and my father lovingly picked up toys I'd left lying about and put them away so they'd not be ruined."

Testing? Testing?

Poltergeists seem to be especially fond of messing about with electricity. Many people mention strange actions of house lights, electronic equipment and appliances of all kinds.

Paul Pepper said that his television sometimes comes on spontaneously when he's in another room, but turns off when he goes in to see about it. One time when he especially wanted to see a ghost segment on "Unsolved Mysteries," he set his VCR to record it while he and his dogs had their nightly walk. When he played the tape, he found that it had recorded all of the show *but* the ghost segment.

Many restaurant kitchens are considered haunted, to those who work there, because electrical appliances behave in a quirky manner. Many people are alarmed in their homes because the lights flare up or fade down. Electricians tell us that there are usually practical explanations for such happenings. They say surges of power or faulty switches could account for most such events. But people who tell the stories often say their first thought was of fire danger, so they had wiring inspected or devices checked out and found no defects.

Psychic investigators say that electricity, a subtle as well as a powerful force, is ideally suited for discarnates to manipulate. In fact, it is a part of all of us; even the beating of our hearts is regulated by electrical action. Yet in another way it seems ghosts would resent electricity. Modern lighting, inside and out, leaves them few shadowy corridors and black nights. Our homes are filled with music and human voices, gunfire and deafening crashes. If ghosts want to make themselves known, they surely find it difficult in our noisy world where attention of the living is usually focused on the flickering images of television or computers. Unusual little sounds and tantalizing glimpses of misty figures are not likely to reach us. Maybe poltergeists are the only spirits left who have much chance of being noticed.

'I wouldst be spoke to...'
Poor noble ghost that comes from place of pain...
To tread again in mournful armor clad
Thy soft grey fields upon a winters night.
Thou wouldst be spoke to, for unless one speaks
Thou canst not, must be spoke to then or go
Unheard, uncomforted to misery.
Stevie Smith, *King Hamlet's Ghost*

Chapter Five

Things That Go Bump

From Ghoulies and ghosties
And long leggit beasties
And things that go bump in the night:
Dear Lord, deliver us.

Old Celtic Prayer

These lines from a few centuries ago surely were inspired by the species of spook very noticeable in any collection of ghost stories, those that focus on frightening or puzzling sounds. These range from horrendous blasts that seem to fracture the air to pleasant murmurs or fragments of music or strident human conversation in places where the listener knows such sounds are impossible. This category, too, should perhaps include sensations that bump human consciousness silently. Included could be odors or overpowering sensations of the nearness of evil. And in this class could be the feeling of a light touch from a hand or a pet's paw, or rough pushing or jostling. Missourians have reported some of each.

Case in point for voices: Wildwood Horse Farm near Centralia. One day one of the owners, Terry Frazee, was working in the barn with an associate, Donna Sapp, whose retired show champion, Sir Love Alot, lives at Wildwood. The two people were half the barn's length apart when both heard someone call out "Terry!"

"You're being paged," Donna commented, and Terry stepped to the barn door. From there he expected to see his wife, Lynn, on the porch of their home, but he saw nobody. There was no car in the driveway, which is visible straight to the county road, and nobody was in sight anywhere. He walked to the house where he found Lynn deep in a project, surprised to see him.

Nobody could have driven up to the barn and shouted and driven away again. Frazee and Sapp know nobody who would regard a practical joke as worthy of taking a long walk from the road and hiding behind the barn while Terry went to the house. It had not been a child's voice. It was female, with no particular urgency. Both had assumed Lynn needed Terry's help in some way or wanted to remind him of something. The incident defied logical explanation.

Just Checking In

A similar event occurred with my mother-in-law. My husband and I were starting on a motor trip, to be gone several days, so we stopped at her house first, to make sure there was nothing she needed before we left. She assured us that everything was fine for her and she made her usual affectionate farewell, commending us, as always, to heavenly protection.

That night when my husband made his usual "all's well" phone call to her, he heard a distraught account of his mother's panic through the day. "Less than an hour after you left," she told him, "I heard you call me from the sun room. You said nothing but 'Mom!' the way you do to let me know you're in the house. Just that one word, but I would swear anywhere that it was your voice. When I found nobody was there, I was sure something had happened. I called the hospitals and the highway patrol...."

This lady belonged to a generation that firmly believed "coming events cast their shadows before them" and that anything can be predicted if one only reads the signs right. She had no doubt that hearing her son's voice was warning of tragedy. But because she also knew how some of her descendants regarded such beliefs, she added "I didn't imagine this. I wasn't dozing in my chair or even thinking about you. I was on my feet in the bathroom, getting ready for my hairdresser appointment. Yet I never heard anything more clearly or naturally in my life, than your voice was then."

Owl As Prophet?

One young woman told solemnly of a neighborhood event that affected several families. They have nice homes on a Columbia cul de sac centered on a charming little green/woods, and all were devastated one winter night when a young woman — stranger to all — took her own life there. Their sympathy for her was tempered by regret that the place which had always given them peace would be permanently tainted now with the memory of tragedy.

"But there was one very strange thing about this," the story teller said. "For five nights before the death, a screech owl called out in our little woods. Many of us had lived our lives without ever hearing this call...really eerie, sounding like a lost soul. Most of us thought owls just went 'who? who?' Anyone who heard this in our park alerted others so we could come out and listen and let our children have the experience. Some of us have lived here for many years and never before known of an owl being

in our woods. We are in the center of town, after all, situated between two big and busy streets."

The punch line to this is that the owl was heard no more after the suicide. And a neighbor who is of Cherokee descent told them that to many Native tribes the owl is considered a harbinger of death. Though they respect its beauty, power and stealth, few Native People incorporate its name into their own.

Be Careful What You Start

A Kansas City newspaper called *The New Times* had a story in November, 1993, about a house identified only as "Bob's house" because the family did not want their lives complicated by publicity.

Bob said he felt he had brought their problems on them himself. Having found that when the attic door was slightly ajar, opening a certain other door on the second floor would cause the attic door to rattle, he used that as a ploy to get his children to bed at night, telling them the ghosts were ready to come out.

Not long after Bob started doing this, the family began to experience some poltergeist-like activity. For instance, a bowl of fruit flew off a counter before the eyes of several people and smashed on the floor. More common, though, were worrisome sounds. Scratchings came from inside the walls and though the family tried to attribute these to mice or squirrels, the noise suggested something much bigger and went quickly from place to place all over the house. And how could the sound of water running in the walls be explained when a plumber could find no cause for it and nobody found water damage anywhere?

Bob's family also heard heavy steps going up and down the attic stairs, sometimes pausing so that weary sighs were audible. Fortunately, manifestations never got worse than this. Everyone adapted. They were still in the house when the story was published, and Bob was quoted as saying, "We decided, if it does turn out to be something...it's nothing, if you know what I mean."

The Choking Ghost

One reader told of events in a farmhouse on the Osage River."I think my grandparents moved there in 1897," he said. "My mother was born there in 1900. It was a very nice place for its time, seven rooms with two big porches. It belonged to a doctor who had moved to town and used his farm as rental property."

The farm's large nice-lying acreage was what attracted the story teller's German grandfather, and his being "a hard-headed Dutchman" made him dismiss what the neighbors said. They warned that the place was haunted by the ghost of the doctor's daughter, Lucy, who had died there at fourteen of tuberculosis. It was rumored, they said, that the girl's step-mother was callous to her sufferings and did very little to ease them. The hauntings reportedly began when neighbors were "sitting up" with the girl's body, as was customary then. They said that suddenly, all over the house, came small crashes, as if every window, one by one, slammed down. Only a few days later, they said, the doctor and his second wife moved out of the house, but they denied any unusual reason for going so abruptly.

First sounds the German family heard were in the walls, scrabbling and scratching which, as in Bob's house, moved about rapidly from place to place. At the same time, the sounds seemed too loud for mice or squirrels, especially when they went overhead. There they sounded like some fairly large animal pouncing in play and rolling about. From the ground nobody could see openings big enough for any animal.

Access to the attic from inside was not possible because in wallpapering the house the couple had covered the attic trapdoor which they never expected to need. Tearing that paper off would spoil the looks of the room, so they never saw into the attic until some roof repairs were made. Then they could climb up on ladders and peer in. Even the father admitted there was no evidence of animal occupancy; decades of dust on the floor lay undisturbed.

Before that, however, family members heard increasingly alarming sounds — coughing, choking and gasping. Since, as the practical-minded father kept pointing out, sounds can't hurt anyone, the family adapted, even to the point of joking about them. If the distressed sounds occurred while guests were present, the mother poked the ceiling with a broom stick and ordered Lucy to be still. She usually obeyed.

The local minister was one person who heard Lucy's agonized efforts to breathe and he was much upset, advising the family to move at once. As if in reassurance, organ music began. It was always heard when nobody was near the organ, perhaps on the porch or tending flower beds or otherwise occupied outdoors. Even when they locked all doors but the one they used as exit and could see from where they were, the music continued.

Only a few times did anyone see anything in the house. Once when a child was sick and the mother was sleeping with it, she said she awakened to see a white figure seated on the edge of the bed. Putting out her hand, she implored, "What have I done? Why won't you stop pestering us?" The figure slowly rose to the ceiling and disappeared.

A maiden aunt who was a member of this family said that she too had seen a white figure, as did one of the grandmothers, visiting while she recovered from malaria. The father pointed out, as today's ghost experts do, that anything seen when one is sick and feverish, should be discounted. The same goes, we're told, for whatever seems to occur during our minds' tricky state between sleeping and waking.

The German family left the haunted house in 1906 with the father still maintaining that what the others claimed to have seen and heard was all nonsense. However, his wife said he was not nearly as firm as he had been and she believed he had experienced something he would not admit.

Granny's Perfume

Sometimes a very bad odor, or a pleasant one is a feature of a haunting, as *Missouri Ghosts* recounted in the case of Lilac Hill, near Fayette. And at Skyrim Farm near Columbia, a smell that mixed attractive and repellent qualities often seemed to foreshadow some misfortune among the horses. What she called "the sweet burning" alerted owner Alice Thompson and her partner, Dick Cook, to take particular care.

A detailed account of a spiritual contact by odor came from Tim Lowery, Independence. A few years ago he lost a grandmother who had been very dear to him. Though not much experienced with bereavements, he instinctively did something grief therapists advocate: he wrote about his feelings. He composed a poem to his mother for a Mother's Day gift. The poem described his grief for his grandmother and the renewed gratitude it gave him for the mother he still had.

Sitting in the floor of his home, Tim read his poem aloud, hardly able to read for crying, but he managed to struggle through it. His reward, he says, was a sudden strong wafting of his grandmother's perfume. "Sort of rosy," is his description, "...with clean country things added, and there was something in the air, whiteness and

sparkly stuff." He felt that the aroma came through his
north wall and left the same way, but it remained for
several minutes, then gradually faded away and seemed
to be followed out by an influx of gently moving air.

While the scent lasted, Tim found himself asking his
grandmother wordlessly but, with great intensity, if she
was all right, and felt her replying that she was fine, and
so was his grandfather and so was Tim's dog, Aussie,
who had died about 18 months earlier. She also seemed
to convey to Tim that she and her husband were very
proud of him.

Tim emphasizes that he said nothing aloud except
the poem, and that his grandmother's reply came directly
into his mind. "I cried and cried," he says, even though
feelings of peace and love came from the experience.
This was exactly the feeling, he always had when going
to his grandmother for help with problems or with a
triumph or pleasure to share. The incident, Tim says,
changed his feelings about death for all time.

One Last Call

Paul Pepper of Columbia lost his mother a few years
ago and he tells of something unforgettable that happened as he moved the last of her belongings into his
own home for sorting and dispersal to various friends
and relatives. He was starting down the basement steps
with a box that contained, among other things, his
mother's telephone. This had special meaning for him
because her home had been in another town and phone
calls had been a precious link between them.

As he descended to his basement, the telephone,
uncharged for six months, rang clearly and loudly. "This
was not the kind of jangle you might expect from its
being dropped or jostled around, Pepper says. "It had
been moved around all day, carried down stairs in St.

Louis, put into the car, taken out of the car, carried over driveway and lawn. If it was just movement, why didn't any of that activity make it ring?"

Did Paul answer the ring? "Yes," he says, "Instinctively, I did." There was, of course, no response, but the telephone figured in a comforting dream in which his mother called to tell him she was still nearby and would help him through his bereavement.

As For Us

"What about your own experiences?" readers often ask, assuming that whomever researches the supernatural must have been inspired by ghostly encounters of her own.

I can recall little that even remotely qualifies, unless a legitimate niche exists for olfactory hallucinations. During college days, I once smelled gas so strongly in the night that I woke others up; they could smell nothing and the house did not explode, then or later. Once when I was in the woods alone, at least a mile from any house, I enjoyed several minutes' aroma of brownies baking too much, in the stage where they develop delectable crusty edges. Only effect was to make me go home and bake brownies.

Another experience I've never stopped wondering about was the recurrent smell of bacon frying. The first time, the odor was so pervasive and lasting that I went to the kitchen to see if some burglar was having a snack before leaving. The bacon smell came several more times, always when I was awakened by my neighbor returning home at four o'clock or so from coon hunting. It infuriated me that I had to listen to the welcoming chorus of hounds who hadn't been allowed to go, a lot of banging of his tail gate as he unloaded his gear and dogs, then gushing water and rattling feed pans as he took care of the animals' needs before going inside. I knew that my neighbor would have a big breakfast, then lie down for a couple of hours sleep before going to work. But both our houses were shut up and his kitchen was in the middle of his house on the side away from ours. There was no way I could smell what he was cooking.

Once, after a visit with a friend, I found my car thick with the smell of my father. He had been gone for years; my friend and I had not been talking about him and I'd had no particularly strong thoughts about him that day; he had never been in my car and I'd been in no car with him since my childhood. Yet there it was, whiskey, Bull Durham tobacco, sun-dried chambray shirt and other indefinable elements of a personal odor I had always loved. It had been associated for me with distribution of money and comic books, solutions for problems, and interesting conversation. I sat and inhaled my father's scent for as long as it lasted, thankful for what seemed like a little visit. My psychic friends would tell me that was exactly what it was, but if my father initiated it, why then? Why not soon after his death when it would have been so comforting to be able to think he was still around?

Adele Graham, illustrator of this book and others, says she has had several thought-provoking little experiences, never of any later significance, seldom dramatic. This is typical:

"I had a cat named Mau, who lived an exceptionally long life with my family. He was very beautiful and we all considered him highly intelligent. Often, after his death, I felt Mau joining me on the couch when I nap there. On the bed at night, I sometimes still feel his weight as usual, pulling covers tight over my feet.

"One of his habits was that he regularly sought out my car keys to play with. He often reminded me in this way that I'd left them in an unusual place and saved me the trouble of a frantic search next morning.

"Only a few weeks ago, I had left my keys lying on the couch; I knew they were here, but some hours into the evening, here came the familiar jingle. How can we explain this, since the keys had been lying there for hours and nobody was up walking around to jar the floor or the couch?"

Not long ago, Adele says, her mother, Shannon, having just washed her hair, reached out blindly for a towel she'd left conveniently on the counter. Instead, it felt as if her fingers had met the familiar curves of Mau's head. When Shannon looked, there was nothing on the counter but the towel.

It would be easy to dismiss all such stories as evidence of human power to create private sensations for emotional comfort. But that doesn't explain incidents that seem unrelated to happenings past or subsequent. Surely if visual hallucinations are possible then olfactory or aural or tactile hallucinations must be possible too. Everything seems to go back to one conclusion: a great deal remains for human beings to figure out.

Like steps of passing ghosts,
The leaves, frost crisped,
Break from the trees and fall.
Adelaide Crapsey

Chapter Six

Four-Footed Phantoms

*In my opinion, sufficient evidence is at
hand to prove for all practical purposes that
animals, as well as humans, survive death.*
Raymond Bayless, *Animal Ghosts*

We don't often think of animals as being haunters or
hauntees, but apparently Missouri has always had some
of each. Vance Randolph, in his book, *Ozark Magic and
Folklore*, told several stories of ghostly creatures. They
were often sinister black dogs — usually of remarkable
size, sometimes headless — who harassed cattle or
hunters or solitary night-time travelers. People claimed
to have struck at some of these specters with a stick or
whip and seen the weapon pass through their bodies.

The *Old Settler's Digest* told of a ghostly horse and
buggy that clattered over covered bridges, its way lit by
lanterns that seemed to be wrapped in fog. In *Missouri
Ghosts* I repeated one of Randolph's best stories, about a
horse and buggy doctor who had often, in a certain
neighborhood, been joined for a mile or so by a large
black dog who would run alongside, then disappear. The
doctor assumed this was some lonely farm dog who just
enjoyed "going a piece" with passersby. He assumed this

until the time, when crossing a stream, he happened to look back and saw that his companion was not swimming or fording; the dog was walking on the surface of the water!

Our own noisy and brightly lighted times are not conducive to ghostly activity, and we're so detached from the natural world that we're less likely than our forebears to notice unusual happenings with animals, but we do have a few good stories. One stars a rabbit, a few star cats and several star dogs or horses. Some of these are inextricably tied to other haunts and appear in other chapters, for instance, the Hallsville rabbit in chapter four and the Southern Horses in chapter fourteen. Here are others.

What Happened to Bruce?

One animal who seemed to see or experience something upsetting was Bruce, a mature German Shepherd who belonged to the Joe Jeff Davis family, owners for several years of the historic Fayette house called Lilac Hill. This house and its dog are part of my earlier book, *Missouri Ghosts*. Bruce bears repeating.

Reared in the family and devoted to the Davis children, Bruce had always been an inside-outside dog, but at Lilac Hill, he could not be kept out. Even when the children were gone to school, he would reappear, sometimes only minutes after being evicted. Marsha Davis didn't mind having Bruce's company, actually, when she was alone in the house with her baby.

One day, hearing a sound — small and distressed — that was unlike any of those usual to the house, she followed it into the former owner's bedroom. This room was furnished with some of that woman's belongings; the Davises had even bought a fragile old velvet bedspread that had lain on the bed for decades. They did not use the room themselves. Lilac Hill provided plenty of space for their children and for guests.

To her surprise, Marsha found Bruce in the center of the bed, glassy eyed and whimpering, the precious spread clawed into a lump of ruin beneath him. All around was slimy gelatinous green material, as if he'd been very sick after eating something very strange. Every aspect of the picture was puzzling. Bruce had been taught from puppyhood to stay off furniture and never violated the rules. This bed was higher than average, so it would have taken some effort to get up there. Why would a sick dog do that instead of crawling under the bed, or more likely, coming to the people he knew would help him?

Veterinarians questioned about this had little insight to offer. Antifreeze could produce green vomit, but no dog would survive ingesting it. Eating the "scours" of calves who were sick from eating the first watery grass of spring might produce similar vomit, but it was not that time of year. Besides, Bruce had been in the house all day. At least Marsha thought he had. So what might the green stuff be besides vomit?

"It took the poor old fellow more than half an hour to look like himself again," she says "and he stayed close to me for the rest of the day." The incident suggests, of course, that Bruce had some sort of encounter — chased something onto the bed or sensed something in a room he seldom entered and had a taxing confrontation there.

Nothing unusual ever happened to Bruce again so far as the family knew; he lived several more years, dying after the Davises had left Lilac Hill.

Homecoming

The late Russ Hawkins, Ashland's well known collector of ghost stories, had one about some dogs — a "fiest" and a large retriever — whose faithfulness extended beyond death.

It seems that a prosperous Missouri farmer had a son who was either a chronic invalid or disabled in some way. On the boy's request or because the father wanted to provide a treat for his son, an extensive European trip was arranged. Unable to take time off from work to oversee the trip himself, the farmer hired someone else to do it, a well-traveled man, aware of the best places to go, the best routes and hotels. A further measure of the father's indulgence: the boy's two beloved dogs went along.

The father received several letters from his son, delighted with the voyage and with all he was seeing. But then the letters stopped. We can only guess what measures the farmer tried to take to locate his son and the traveling companion. No doubt all involved recognized it as a lost cause. The companion had murdered or abandoned the boy for the money involved.

What convinced the father that there was no hope was the dogs' return — sort of. Both he and his employees saw them, close enough to have no doubt of their identity, but never near enough to touch them. The dogs were seen in all their usual places outdoors, fairly often at first, but less and less until they appeared no more. To the father it seemed intended as a message, but he was not sure what the message meant. That the dogs had been killed, freeing them to return in this way, but the boy was still alive? Or that all were gone to another realm of existence and the dogs had come back to hint to the father of that and then had returned to their young owner?

The Dogs All Knew

Sue Webster told me that her father had a tradition of calling his five children each Sunday evening, just for a brief check-in to see if all was well. He usually reached Sue around eight p.m. One particular Sunday, she and her husband were watching TV in the company of their large dog, a mixture of bold breeds whose warnings could be taken seriously.

This night their pet stalked to the patio doors growling, but her tone quickly changed to something more like a whine and she came and pressed herself hard against them, trembling. She continued to tremble for several minutes, and look uneasily at the doors. Her owners could see nothing there.

Half an hour or so later, Sue's mother called to tell them that Sue's father had died suddenly at church. Back home with her siblings for their father's funeral, Sue mentioned her dog's behavior, noting that it happened almost exactly at the time of the death. One by one the others related, with amazement, that their dogs had reacted in similar ways. The sister who had several collies, their father's favorite breed, said her dogs circled the house, running and barking.

Another little experience Sue cherishes: her father, in the days of Lassie's prominence on TV, greatly enjoyed the show and was pleased to know somebody who won a Lassie puppy in a naming contest. The winning name had been "Friend" and Sue says her father often commented on what a good name that was, more dignified than Buddy or Pal, reminding everyone who heard it of a dog's true worth. He later had a dog whom he called Friend.

Sue's son, Matt, never knew his grandfather, and nothing had been said to him about a dog named Friend. The child was very fond of a pull-along toy dog, and one day Sue said to him, "What's your puppy's name?" "It's Friend," the toddler replied at once. "His name is Friend."

The Dog Cinched It

In Nevada, Jack and Shirley Ann Bastow bought a nice old house which had been allowed to fall into ruin. With love and care, ignoring local warnings about the place's "colorful history", they restored it to much the appearance it had when new. The builder had been a successful Nevada merchant named John Clack. He and his wife, Delia, took eleven years to build, so they must have incorporated all the dream-home fantasies each of them entertained. Patrick Brophy, writing about it in his engrossing history of Vernon County, *Past Perfect*, knew of nothing untoward that had happened there except that Delia died at a younger than average age. However, this was not before she saw their daughter make a desirable marriage, into which she was beautifully launched from the parlor of her parents' home.

While working on the house, the Bastows experienced nothing more annoying or unpleasant than tools disappearing, but after living there awhile, they began to hear quarrelsome voices in parts of the house distant from where they happened to be. They could never find evidence of prankster entry. Another puzzling episode was a woman reported relaxing on their back deck when they were away on vacation. A friend passing by, aware that they were gone, did not know what to think about a woman in dark clothes sitting there as if she owned the place.

As time passed and nothing harmful happened to them or their property, the Bastows began to feel on rather friendly terms with their ghosts and to joke about them in conversation. Guests in their home were always intrigued by Shirley Ann's custom of leaving an open Bible in each room. She had read that this is a good ploy for keeping ghosts away, and had tested it by sometimes closing the books. When she did, strange things happened again. And one of the strangest was this:

The couple's aging dog had never liked the house, showing great uneasiness when they first moved in, but gradually adjusting. He had one adventure that nobody ever could begin to explain. On a morning after a night of heavy rain, with thunder and lightening, the dog was found to be soaking wet. He had been indoors when the couple locked up and went to bed and all the doors were still locked next morning. Brophy did not comment on whether or not the animal was afraid of storms, but a great many dogs are, especially as they age. There were no leaks or other sources of drenching water in the house. The only possible explanation would seem to be that somebody entered the house for burglary, and the dog went outside when they came in — whether or not he was afraid of storms — then back in when they went out. There was no sign of entry, though. Nothing was missing or disturbed, and the dog had not barked as almost any dog would do if its domain were invaded.

Oops, Mitzi! Sorry!

LeAnn Gilbert, who was born in Rolla and now lives in Sand Springs, Oklahoma, had a grey-blue cat named Mitzi who shared her home for many years. When the much-cherished cat died, LeAnn had trouble adjusting to the loss, even though she still had Mitzi's companion, another Russian Blue named Tyrell. Mitzi was often in

LeAnn's dreams, and several times, she told her family, she had glimpses of the lovely cat. Sometimes Tyrell, who had lost his vision, went through the actions she and Mitzi had followed in play, actions that one cat would not do alone.

Of course LeAnn found little acceptance for her contention that Mitzi was still around, not until an evening when friends came over to play cards. One of the men excused himself to go to the bathroom. When he came out, all present heard a crash that reverberated loudly in the hallway. The friend joined them in apologetic mode.

"LeAnn," he said, "I may have stepped on Tyrell. I fell into the wall trying to avoid him, but those grey cats are so hard to see. He ran off, and now I can't find him!"

"Roy," Lee Ann said, lifting Tyrell up for all to see. "He's been in my arms the whole time." She didn't have to say, "Now to you believe me about Mitzi?"

Hooved Haunts

And now for the supernatural and horses. One man talking to me at a book signing said that when he was a young farm boy he was one day working alone while his father and their hired man replaced the gates to a large field. They were out of sight of the boy.

"Around noon," he said, "a party of horsemen rode in and stopped to rest under a big tree by our stream. This was nothing unusual. We were glad for people to refresh themselves there. But there wasn't a single guy or horse that I knew in the group and there was something odd about them. Ordinarily I'd have gone over and talked, but they didn't return my wave, so I just went on working. As I think of their clothes now, it seems like there was a lot of blue mixed in, like remnants of Union uniforms. I've always thought there was something supernatural about this. Now I wonder if they were from another time."

The visitors loosened girths and let their horses drink and graze. Some of the men splashed water on their own heads and faces. They broke out food. The observer couldn't see what they were eating, but he noted that they made no fire. "They rested for maybe 45 minutes," he said, "then gathered up and rode out again, just as anyone would do who stopped there."

At supper, the boy asked his father if he knew who the horsemen were and why they seemed so strange. The father declared that nobody had ridden by him that day. How could several horses and riders pass unnoticed while he and his employee worked on the gate? Not wanting to appear demented, the boy never mentioned the incident again, but as an aging man he told me, "I remember it as clearly as if it were a movie I saw last night. I remember that one of the horses was spotted and I'd seen very few spotted horses up to then. Nobody in our area had one."

Did It Come True On Him?

In St. Louis in 1991, Deanna Bruno wrote of a Chesterfield area hermit named Johann Kuhschwanz who loved to ride his white horse around on side streets and roads at night to scare people. Whether he wore some special outfit for his nocturnal excursions was not specified, nor was it known whether he had the horse trained to rear or do other fearsome things. But she wrote that one night the horse came tearing down one of the busier streets of town, dragging its owner, who seemed to be clinging to its tail. Neither of them was ever seen again.

The Wildest Ride

A Mexico woman told of a really wild ride: in her country community, since before she was born, people talked of a ghost inhabiting a certain deserted little church. It appeared as an emaciated old woman with flying white hair and always naked. Nobody suggested anything worse than just seeing her, but on a stormy night one horseman had an extremely close encounter. He had taken refuge in the church, but because of its reputation, he stood barely inside the vestibule, holding his horse's reins. He was resolved not to look behind him, or to left or right.

However, the ghost announced herself with a shrill laugh that could not be ignored. A lightning flash revealed the apparition he'd heard of all his life. Helped by adrenaline, the man jumped onto his horse and spurred it away from the church door. To his horror, the next lightning flash revealed the old woman, ravaged, flabby and grinning crazily, perched behind his saddle. The story does not say whether he could feel her holding onto his body or his clothes; it does not say whether she went all the way home with him, or how the horse reacted to such goings on.

Hag-rid Horses

A February 13, 1902, clipping from vertical files of the state historical society in Columbia, refers to a superstition about "hag-rid" horses. The author, a Cooper Countian named I. McDonald DeMuth, told of a day in 1860 when he was saddling his favorite mare for a trip to town and one of his father's stable employees came and earnestly entreated him not to take her out. The man warned that less than a week earlier the mare had undoubtedly been hag-ridden because she was found one morning to be exhausted, sweat-crusted and nervous. Though she was recovering, she still could not be trusted to behave normally.

The stable man went ahead to explain that hags are little creatures about a foot tall who look like "a shriveled, skinny old woman" except that they have wings similar to a bat's and their feet and hands are like the feet of raptors, equipped with strong claws. These creatures slip up on sleeping horses and by digging in talons and flapping their wings, terrorize the poor animals into giving them an exciting ride. Proof positive, which he showed the boy, is that the abused horse's mane, which the hags use to steer by, will next day hang in tight twists, fastened together at the ends with cockleburs.

DeMuth had figured out, by the time he wrote, that this was a ruse invented in hope of excusing employees who had borrowed one of their employer's horses for an evening of courting or charging about with friends and then left the poor creature standing in its sweat all night. The legend, if they could sell it, would explain any damage they might have done to the animal with spurs, or by running it into something or making it jump.

It was not so easy for DeMuth to figure out the tangled mane, the seemingly woven strands still called "witch locks" or "witch braids" and very tedious to separate and make brushable. Horse people patiently do it, in order not to lose hair — thus beauty — from their animals' manes. DeMuth decided that a horse picks up one or more cockleburs, which scratch and prick the animal as they swing around in the long hair of the mane. The horse rubs against a tree or fence post trying to get rid of the burr and in the process sets up static electricity which weaves the hair together. Nice thinking for 1902, perhaps, but not much help in dealing with today's witch locks!

Is Jewell Psychic?

Jewell is a beautiful American Saddlebred brood mare who lives at Wildwood Farm near Centralia. She is very attached to her owner, who comes regularly to see her, though she no longer rides Jewell. Despite her loving disposition, the mare is what horsepeople call "hot," not a relaxing ride. Jewell has unusually large, expressive eyes and other unique characteristics.

Lynn Frazee, who operates the farm with her husband, Terry, describes Jewell as "the most verbal horse I've ever been around. She has a lot to say about everything." Lynn's daughter, Heather, expands on that. "Sometimes when you're working around her, she keeps up a conversation with varied tones and inflections."

Jewell's partners in conversation include her unborn foals, though this in itself is not uncommon. Many pregnant mares turn their faces back close to their bellies and make tender, cozy little sounds that horsepeople treasure. "You'll never hear that except when they've pregnant or have new babies," they explain. Lynn says that Jewell's prenatal murmurings are more constant than any mare she's ever seen, but Jewell goes farther.When pregnant women come into the barn, she tries to get to them so she can "listen" to their bellies and say a few words. She did this daily while Heather was pregnant.

When Jewell's owner conceived, everyone was touched, as time passed, to see Jewell's intense interest. She sometimes talked to the woman's belly loudly enough to disrupt human conversations. Admittedly, two people who love Jewell may have read delight into her reactions, but they wondered if the mare realized this was a fragile pregnancy. Special measures were being taken to preserve it.

One day, after a week of being unable to visit Jewell, the owner appeared and the mare came to her at once. This time, however, though Jewell put her face closer than ever, she did not make a sound. Lynn recalls feeling, at that moment, forebodings she did not express, and a day later, learned the reason. Her friend's baby had died. All realized that Jewell had known. As this chapter was written, the friends were anticipating Jewell's reaction when her owner appears with a recently born baby.

So what was really going on with Jewell, Bruce and the others? Lynn, who grew up in a horse-training barn and loves all animals, analyzes it this way: "They just know things — feel things — that are beyond us. Maybe we could too, if we weren't so involved in so much, if our senses weren't so overloaded."

Haunted Places

For over all there hung a cloud of fear,
a sense of mystery the spirit daunted,
and said as plain as whisper in the ear,
"The place is haunted."

Thomas Hood

The declaration above applies to a great many places in Missouri. Some are well-documented as harboring something unusual and others are merely said, without details, to be haunted. Still others, by their history, appearance or atmosphere seem to need ghosts. In the next few chapters, we'll look at some in each of these categories. But we'll start with something that may be unique to Missouri — a haunted town. A distinction needs to be made between a haunted town and a ghost town; the latter term usually refers merely to a town that has been deserted, often with a surprising number of human possessions left behind. Ronnie Powell's home town, in which he still lives, seems to be very haunted. An article of his which appeared in *Country Folk Magazine* starts this section which then continues with accounts, from various sources, of other haunted places.

Chapter Seven

The Ghosts of Windyville

by Ronnie Powell

Highway K strays from State Road 64 south four miles to Windyville, Missouri, where it unexpectedly enters the small Ozark town, then crosses the Niangua River a mile or so on. It turns westward between Four Mile Creek and the river into hills of forest and deep hollows and emerges at last into Highway 32. In late spring and summer, Black Eyed Susan and Queen Anne's Lace crowd the roadside, nodding to those who pass, and like dream catchers, spider webs glisten between strands of rusty barbed wire fence. Only a small road sign, obscured somewhat by cedar boughs, marks the north boundary of Windyville, allowing just seconds to glimpse the village as one passes through.

The road rushes between two old store buildings, fronted by the Moon Valley Road and Highway M. The smallest building is vacant, its weathered front faded, draped with vine and shadowed by the canopy of a huge elm. Across from it stands the Windyville General Store, a large, stately structure with a high false front where faded letters proclaim its beginning in 1921.

The spacious old store has changed little in its 75 years; only its owners have changed. A short distance behind the store is an old tomato canning factory, a relic of the depression era. A rusty tin roof, loose in many places, covers most of the weary structure. It is isolated, windowless and holds many secrets within its perpetual darkness. A post office and small antique store are located approximately fifty feet east of the store. Seven dwellings and a community building complete the cross-road town.

Most people who pass through Windyville would never guess what bizarre occurrences have plagued the town and surrounding area over the years. Much of it has become legend, passed down — often reluctantly — by descendants of those who experienced the frightful happenings. But time has not erased their memory. Some people scoff at the idea that the supernatural often comes at night to haunt the innocent. Others are skeptical, but all are ill at ease, uncertain of their convictions.

It has been speculated that desecrated graves of Osage Indians, numerous in and around Windyille, are in part the cause of the many mysterious happenings. Like other Native Tribes, the Osage Indians of the Niangua River Basin had sacred rituals, ceremonies and customs which demonstrated their sincere belief in a supreme being, a hereafter and also in evil spirits. As exiles from their ancestral land, Osage people were forbidden to return to the burial sites to pay homage as their culture demanded. The burial of their dead has been defiled countless times over and skeletal remains sometimes appear in this area in plowed fields, hog yards and cattle lots.

It is not just the Osages who believe that the spot where a person is laid to rest never forgets and that the person in some ways is still there and can actually partake of a living being's spirit and breath. Some Windyville stories:

🕊 A mile or so south of town there once stood a house besieged by unexplained events in and around it. Rocks were said to fall suddenly from the ceiling or from the trees outside. Many claimed to have witnessed the phenomenon. Before this, the owner of the house disappeared without a trace and it was believed that his wife and her lover killed him and hid his body in a cave on the Niangua.

🕊 In a house at the center of Windyville, across from the general store, a young boy was badly frightened by loud wailing in a second story room. His parents told him that it was only his imagination, but later one night it came again. The boy's father learned that an old man had passed away in that room several years before, after suffering dreadfully from a mysterious illness. A few years later, the father himself, while standing on the back porch one night, felt a heavy hand come to rest on his shoulder. When he turned to see who it was, nobody was there.

🕊 In 1994 after a local woman's untimely death, her ghostlike image appeared briefly in the house. She was the picture of youth again, clear of skin, with flowing raven hair hanging to her hips and she wore a long orange dress.

🕊 The old canning factory has not been spared in the haunting of Windyville, for there have been claims of frightful screams and loud pounding from its shadowy interior. Once a man repairing a nearby fence decided to take a look inside the building. A door that had long since given up its hinges stood partly ajar near the north end of the building. He carefully picked it up and placed it against a tree.

Inside, the only light was from a waning sun, streaming through cracks in the walls. Littering the floor were empty tomato crates and brown glass jugs. Dust lay heavy over all the debris but not a track of animals or humans was evident anywhere.

Above him the explorer could see a loft, half the width of the building and at one end a ladder ascended to the darkness above. Still at ease and curious, he started up but stopped abruptly when he heard what sounded like shuffling footsteps overhead.

"It sounded," the man said, "as if someone was trying to creep toward the edge of the loft." Not one to frighten easily, he scrambled up the ladder and peered around, expecting to confront somebody or some creature.

"Light was poor," the man continued, "but I could see the entire length and breadth of the loft and nothing was there, not even a track to mar the dust on the floor. I guess I lost it then," he laughed, "for I flung myself down the ladder and ran for the doorway. But when I got there, I found the door had been placed against the opening. I'll tell you one thing for sure; I didn't waste any time busting through to the outside and I've not been back since."

One Sunday morning two people observed a small tin bucket hanging on a peg in the front display room of the antique store banging violently against the wall. It continued its erratic movement for nearly five minutes.

Several times heavy footsteps have been heard in the attic above the store, along with the scraping sounds of something being moved.

An aged woman living in a house next door to the store reported that she several times was visited by small children, unfamiliar to her in this small town where everyone knew everyone. The children never uttered a word, but ran about pilfering her belongings. One night, she said, she saw a group of men killing another on the front lawn and for many nights afterwards, she claimed she saw them hiding behind trees watching the house. Most people considered her demented.

In the spring of 1992, another woman of senior years was sitting in a chair on her front lawn, directly behind the antique store, drinking a cup of coffee. She said a blue bird began singing in a tree above her. Delighted by the sweet sound she listened, but said, "At first the sound was that of a bird, but then there were words. It was a sad song of a lost love and I wept."

A stranger wandered into town one morning in the spring of 1993, weary and haggard from a chilly night, lost in the woods. He claimed to have no idea of where he was and wanted only to return home to Springfield. He said that he had spent the night huddled beneath a huge oak tree and that demons leaped from the trees and danced around him. "They taunted me," he said, "and they stank like no creature I have ever known."

When I asked if he had been drinking, the young man looked me straight in the eyes and replied, "No sir. I am a Christian. You must believe me. May God have mercy on all of you, for those creatures are everywhere."'

Another stranger passing through Windyville in late summer of 1993, said the town was disturbingly full of spirits. When asked how he knew, he said, "There is an unearthly coldness here and I can feel them."

A child walking with a parent along the south road that leads out of Windyville suddenly burst into a fit of tears, pointed at a vacant house near the side of the road and cried, "There are ghosts in there!" The house the little girl had so tearfully referred to has suffered the most. Occurrences there have struck terror in many of its occupants and sent them fleeing.

Footsteps on the stairs in the middle of the night finally entered a bedroom to reveal the ghost of a man who once resided in the house. Spiders by the thousands suddenly invaded the house, only to disappear and be replaced by a equal number of cockroaches. Strange pale faces appear at the windows and footsteps hurry away leaving no tracks. The ghost of the man who once lived in the house has also been reported seen in front of the store in broad daylight, once entering a closed window.

For awhile the house was vacant and sometimes in the evening about dusk a curtain would flutter part way open in a second story window. It has also been reported that a coldness often settled in around the house in late evening and would chill the bones of anyone who ventured too close. Once a stench emitted from the house. Neighbors likened it to rotting flesh and the same smell was said to have come — just a few days after his death — from the grave of the man who had once lived in the house.

🐦 In the spring of 1994, all the birds in a portion of Windyville disappeared and did not return until the autumn of the same year. Not even a sparrow could be seen, yet a few hundred feet outside the affected area, birds flourished.

🐦 Sometime in the year of 1934, two young women walking along a road near the Lone Rock Cemetery, a couple of miles west of Windyville, said a cold burst of wind suddenly swept out of the graveyard, scattering leaves and other debris across the road where they stood. Seconds later a horse and rider rose up from near the center of the cemetery to approximately fifty feet above and hovered there motionless for a few seconds. The rider raised an arm and appeared to be shouting. As quickly as it had appeared, the image vanished. Sighting of this horse and rider had been claimed for several years prior to that of the young women. Nobody seems to know why. No sighting has been reported since.

As promised, I have identified no one who revealed to me their stories of ghosts, spirits or otherwise unexplainable events in and around Windyville. Many scoff and say there is no truth in it all, but there are many who believe.

(Windyville, no longer on most road maps, is between Buffalo and Bennett Springs. Powell says the unusual name is believed to have been chosen for its descriptiveness. The town is on top of the second or third highest point in Dallas county.)

Now, some other haunted places....

The Haunted Smithy

Jim Longo, in his two fascinating collections of ghost stories in our state and Illinois — *Haunted Odyssey* and *Ghosts Along the Mississippi* — offers several that are more than unique; one concerns a haunted blacksmith shop. Longo tells us that his subject described buying property in the Femme Osage Valley, the area where Daniel Boone and his son Nathan and other family members had settled. This land included some log buildings from the Boone era, never used by anyone but the builder and his descendants. Among these was a smithy, a necessity for most pioneers because, living so far from town, they usually were on their own for horse shoeing and implement repair.

Longo's source, whom we'll call Carl, for convenience, said that when he was younger, he traveled quite a lot because his own neighborhood didn't provide enough customers to support his family. One night when he came home, his wife told him the anvil had been ringing all day, as if he were at work. The story does not specify if she asked whether he'd given someone else permission to use his equipment, or if they both feared someone was just confiscating it. Those would seem to be the logical first thoughts, yet the wife must have gone out to see what was going on and become uneasy when she found the smithy empty.

As time passed, the farrier said he began to see movement in the smithy and equipment seemed bewitched. Tools and finished work constantly fell from wall hangers that had always previously held them securely. Tools were frequently moved from the logical storage spot to somewhere less convenient.

One day, however, when he had a lot of work to get out and the ghostly impediments were especially bad,

Carl lost his temper and shouted, "Why don't you leave me alone?" Promptly a heavy ox bow (yoke) fell from its well-supported place in the rafters, an object heavy enough to give a fatal head injury. Carl then shouted with even more wrath, challenging the entity to give him a little help sometimes.

Amazingly, from that point, Carl said he not only had fewer problems, he seemed to be helped in dealing with unusual demands of his work. When asked to do something new and difficult, a skillful ally seemed to be advising him. Carl decided he was host to the ghost of a blacksmith or farrier and he concluded, "Whatever it was, it wasn't scary." Carl is far from being the first person to decide that a discarnate companion was friendly, thus making it possible to take all manifestations in stride.

The Haunted Goldenrod

At least two separate sets of ghosts are attributed to the *Goldenrod Showboat*, which is docked at St. Charles and serves as a dinner theater. Those who write about the ghosts aboard usually focus on a young woman named Victoria, drawn to her romantic story.

The apparent basics on Victoria: she grew up on the *Goldenrod*, daughter of a widower captain. He was a totally indulgent father except on one score: he would not tolerate Victoria's dream of becoming one of the boat's dancers. They had a major quarrel over the issue and she flounced off into the night. Next day her body was found floating in the river, wearing a garish red dress nobody had ever seen her in before. Supposition was that she'd found a job dancing in a cheap place where she met misfortune. The devastated father died not long after and the *Goldenrod's* staff began seeing a lady in red whom they at first supposed was a real person. Sometimes she appeared in photos taken by guests or the boat's publicity people and thus the idea of a ghost on the *Goldenrod* was born.

A high school girl named Veronica Villareal, who had worked on the *Goldenrod* as a hostess confirmed to Longo that strange things did happen there. They were mainly the routine haunted places events — unexplainable sounds, objects disappearing and lights turning themselves on.

Veronica's own most unsettling experience came on an evening when she went aboard to pick something up. At that time of night, lights should have been on and the public address system busy with music and with communications from one part of the boat to another. Instead, all was silent and she found herself alone.

Understandably, Veronica hurried through her duties, one of which involved visiting the office. It too was empty and silent. She scuttled off as soon as she could and when she had reached the shore, saw lights come on and music begin, full force. Someone was aboard after all. Next day, when she mentioned the experience to her bosses, they looked at her strangely and said they had all been in their usual places, doing their usual work, the whole time.

Veronica directed Longo to another former employee who said that everyone learned to respect Victoria's spirit after an incident in the galley. A cook, having a bad day blamed it on the ship's close quarters, cursing the Goldenrod. To his surprise, the equipment and the culinary creation he had worked hard on flew across the room, to destruction.

This may have inspired the idea that Victoria loved and protected the *Goldenrod*. Certainly something did, for it survived an era when the average lifespan of a riverboat — according to one of Robbi Courtaway's sources for her book *Spirits of St. Louis* — was about five years, considering all the dangers from its own steam, from flood, storms, snags and fire. Veronica's theory was that Victoria found it easy to live on the *Goldenrod* because it was kept as it looked in the era of her fleshly tenure there.

People who have lived with congenial ghosts often tell researchers that on leaving the haunted area, they feel compelled to bid the entity goodbye. The floor manager Veronica introduced Longo to told him she chose to say good-bye in the banquet room, one of the most beautiful parts of the *Goldenrod*, and the place where she felt Victoria might be most likely to hear her.

Missouri Life and other Missouri publications have explored the Goldenrod exhaustively. Troy Taylor, who publishes *Ghosts of the Prairie* magazine, and runs a large bookstore of supernatural materials, spent time on the *Goldenrod* making a film for the Education Channel. This is available on video from 1-888-Ghostly.

Science tells us that nothing in nature, not even the tiniest particle, can disappear without a trace. Think about that for a moment. Once you do, your thoughts about life will never be the same.

Werner Van Braun

I heard the pastor's words again,
"When the body wears away
like a car and can't go on,
the soul gets out and walks ahead
until it finds its home."
Bee Kuckelman, Columbia,
from her poem, *Bonnie*

Chapter Eight

St. Jo's Ghosts

St. Joseph, one of Missouri's oldest cities, is also one of its most haunted. Having approximately 72,000 residents, St. Jo cannot compete on a per capita basis with Windyville, which Ronnie Powell tells us now has less than a dozen inhabitants. Still, St. Joseph's ghosts are impressive for variety and persistence. This is only to be expected when a city has had more than its share of excitement and striving.

St. Joseph's history goes back to 1790 when a fur company's representative, Joseph Robidoux, established a trading post that became a major rendezvous for trappers and fur traders. In 1834 the city got its name and in 1860 the romantic pony express began there. Famous as "jumping off place" for pioneers heading west, this city built on bluffs overlooking the Missouri River, also bustled for decades with vital steamboat traffic. Great fortunes were earned in St. Joseph, resulting in the building of picturesque mansions, many of which still stand. To all who love old architecture, St. Joseph is one of the most interesting of Missouri's cities. The city also abounds in museums, offering at least ten.

So far, St. Joseph's ghostly history doesn't seem to have been stressed in its publicity, but possibly it should be. In 1989 and in 1993 the *St. Joseph (MO) News-Press Gazette* published full page discussions of the town's

ghosts, never repeating anything. In addition, the library
has a full page photocopy of a similar review published
in the late 30s or early 40s and none of the later stories
derive from this, so the city is rich indeed in ghosts!
Here are some of the most outstanding:

A Multi-Faceted Ghost?

"Mama! Where are you, Mama?" These words, in a
shrill, childlike voice awakened Lois Hughes on the first
night spent in an historic house she and her husband had
just bought. That was only a prelude to what appears to
be activity of either a host of ghosts or one spirit with
wide-ranging abilities. The Hugheses and their daughter,
Jo Anne, soon became familiar with all the standard manifestations — cold spots, sounds from inside walls, footsteps where nobody could be. In addition, they had a
self-playing baby grand piano, and one time, they told
the newspaper reporter, orchestral music came from an
empty room. Another unique event was the arrival of
police, come to investigate screaming that neighbors
reported hearing from the Hugheses upstairs. Lois and
her sister, watching television downstairs, had heard
nothing unusual.

Strangest of all was a figure appearing in pictures
taken on the second floor landing by a magazine photographer doing a feature on the castle-like mansion.
Elsewhere, his work came out as expected, but a series of
shots showing aspects of the lovely, spacious landing
included a filmy figure, gender unclear, which seemed to
move past in front of the camera.

On the advice of a clairvoyant, Lois began keeping
open Bibles and glasses of water in several rooms. This
was supposed to reduce spirit activity and seemed to do
so as long as the objects stayed in place. The clairvoyant

advised that when family members heard voices in remote parts of the house, they should call out, "Begone with you and God bless you."

Though they did not deeply research the history of their house, Lois did learn that it was built in 1890 by James McCallister, a prominent banker. His family left soon, possibly because their two-year old son died there of diphtheria. They had a death mask cast and a sculpted version of this was hung outdoors at the carriage entrance. Lois said each family to occupy the house suffered a death. In her own case, it was her mother. For one couple it was a young son.

During a period in the mid 40s, when the house served as city museum, a local historian named Roy Coy said many puzzling little events occurred. One he recalled most vividly came when he was alone there at night, reading at his desk. From the corner of his eye, he saw the door knob turn and then the door opened completely. Nobody was there and Coy knew nobody else was in the locked-up building that night.

Another time, he and an assistant were working together in the basement when both heard the front door slam and footsteps ascend the main staircase. They knew that the front doors were secured and that nobody else was on duty.

As many other dwellers in houses that appear to be haunted have done, Lois and Ben Hughes developed fondness for their bodiless housemates and told the reporter they would keep the place. Their daughter had asked them to, so she would have it some day. Lois concluded her interview with these words: "We don't call our house haunted. We say it has spirit!"

A Weight-Lifting Ghost?

For about forty years, the staff of St. Joseph's central library has been entertained and inconvenienced by a feisty ghost they call Rosie. Nobody knows who she was, but she does such things as take papers from employees' desks and leave them in the lost and found basket and she's sometimes heard at night clicking over the floor in her high heeled Victorian boots. Some people in the past reported glimpses of a traditional little librarian, hair tightly controlled in a bun, her costume including a long, dark skirt.

For the last few decades, Rosie's most notable performances have been audible but not visible. A custodian working alone after the library was closed, heard light footsteps and went to investigate, thinking perhaps a patron had been inadvertently left inside. He found nobody and returned to work. Soon he heard the footsteps again, accompanied by a woman's laugh. Hurrying back to the spot the noises seemed to come from, he was again disappointed, but then both footsteps and laughter resumed before his eyes. Some library workers have reported wafting flowery scents that they believe is the phantom's perfume.

One of Rosie's feats, however, puts her in an unusual category. An employee who still works at the library reported once seeing a massive old oak card catalog file slowly tip far enough forward that a drawer fell out. This piece of furniture would take a few stout men to move, so what was going on?

A Kansas City psychic called Saphita, whom the 1993 reporter quoted several times, said that spirits which remain earth-bound "may be waiting for something, such as for someone else to die, before they move on. Or they may be guarding something." Perhaps

someday some library employee will discover stored items that give a good clue as to why Rosie is so faithful to her location.

Rockaby Baby

A remarkable ghost story from near Agency, close to St. Joseph, concerned a beautiful baby less than six months old. The child lived with its young parents in a 115-year-old house they had just moved into, a place that the mother said looked like a shack from outside, but had been remodeled and decorated to be quite pleasant and comfortable within. Because their new home was located in a flat open area, the parents were more aware than they had been elsewhere of the sounds of nature — wind, rain, and wildlife. They did not notice for some time that there were unusual sounds inside too.

The couple did find that one of their rooms was strangely cold. Even in moderate weather they often could see their breaths there, and the wife's brother, a young man who ordinarily liked sleeping in unheated rooms, complained when he visited them. Adding a space heater did not much improve the atmosphere.

Another room was plagued with insects. At one time these were crawling creatures, another time those that flew. Once, fat, repulsive grubs floundered around all over the floor. The couple sprayed repeatedly with different products and they stuffed steel wool into all the holes they could find in the boards, but to no avail. All else paled, however, beside the ghostly attention given this couple's baby.

"She was really adorable," her mother said, with no qualifications. "People would stop us on the street to look at her." Perhaps this proud parent was not surprised that even someone on another plane of existence admired her child. She was shocked, however to find that their invisible housemate's regard required uncovering the baby and folding her blanket neatly at the foot of her crib, and this in a cold house.

The reporter did not press the mother for her quiet acceptance of these events. Did she move the baby into her bedroom? Were the viewings on some sort of schedule that made her certain she could visit the child often enough to keep it covered? She was quoted only with "'I knew the men wouldn't do it. I never felt the baby was in danger from this being, but it was weird, you know?"

The couple left the house in a year or so, not because it was haunted, but because of problems with its water system.

Growing Up Haunted

One of the 1989 paper's longest stories was about a 95-year-old house that had been home since childhood for the family's daughter, Nancy, 18 years old when the article was written. The mother said that from the beginning what she termed "chattery" voices came from their daughter's bedroom, presumably before the child was old enough to be there alone. All members of the family heard activity upstairs when Nancy and her sister were away. The father sometimes argued that the girls had to be home when their mother insisted they had gone out for the evening.

Nancy's own descriptions: "I just remember being scared to walk down the hall by myself because you could always feel a presence behind you and sometimes footsteps too." She said, "I'd be lying in my bed and see this figure. It looked like a fat person but not a person like me or you. It was like an outline. The first time I saw it, I didn't go back in my room for a month and for awhile wouldn't even go in there alone in daytime to get my clothes. You could shut a door or be walking through and

shut it behind you and it would open right back up."
Nancy said she felt the ghosts had nothing to do with her
family. "It's their house. They want it back and they're
just trying to scare us out of it."

A feature that may be unique to hauntings involved a
yellow chair Nancy had shared with a deceased cousin
who once lived with the family. "I used it for getting
ready for school in the morning. It was just her favorite
chair. After she died, I could only sit in one side because
it was like there was this person sitting there beside me.
I could never get to the other side of that chair. It was just
like a wall in the middle of it."'

When the St. Joseph newspaper story was written,
this family was still in the house and said nothing about
leaving it. The mother's final word: "We've been frightened, like anyone would be, but I guess you get used to
it."

In the Mirror

On a certain day between 1880 and 1890, a young St.
Joseph woman went to a studio at Third and Felix to have
her picture taken. The photographer directed her to a
small room where she could take off her hat and tidy her
hair before facing the lens. As she entered, the angle of
door and dressing table was such that she saw her own
reflection behind that of another woman who was seated.
This person wore a beautiful but long outdated grey silk
dress and was working with an elaborate hair arrangement. The newcomer murmured an apology, withdrew
and returned to the waiting room. When the photographer sought her out, she explained that she was waiting for
him to attend to his previous customer. He told her he
had no other appointments for the afternoon and went
with her to the dressing room, which they found to be
empty.

That night, the girl told her family of the odd little incident and her mother remembered another story from that building. It had once been rented by a popular dressmaker, but this woman moved out abruptly because of something that happened one afternoon. While she was kneeling on the floor to pin up a customer's hem, the customer suddenly jerked and screamed, and the seamstress jumped to her own feet soon enough to see, for a moment or two, both of them reflected in a mirror behind the image of a woman in a grey dress, working with her hair. Nobody stood between them and the mirror. Nobody else was in the shop. They both left, the customer in her half finished dress, leaving behind the clothing she had arrived in. The seamstress returned later, but only with others to move her belongings to another site.

Eventually, from local memory, the whole story was assembled, and it was a classic of the era: lovely young girl, having fallen in love with someone her family disapproved of, eloped, taking little but the expensive dress she wore. Bitterly dismissed by her parents, she felt she had nowhere to turn when her husband proved to be unreasonable and violent, and when he abandoned her in their paid-up hotel room without money. While starving, she kept up appearances, or perhaps somehow comforted herself, by continuing to maintain her beautiful long hair in its fashionable style.

A neighbor in the hotel had heard shouting and weeping from the room and was relieved when the husband left, but having never been introduced, she was hesitant to approach the wife and of course never dreamed that the young woman might need anything but moral support. When this neighbor finally did knock on the door, she was horrified at the girl's pallor and loss of weight. The food and medical care she provided were too late. She summoned the girl's father and he said he would leave home immediately, but communication and transportation being what it was at the time, his daughter was dead and buried in a pauper's grave before he arrived.

While the father wept in the empty room, the neighbor saw both of them were reflected in the mirror, and with difficulty, considering her own horror, drew his attention to it. For the image of his daughter had joined them. It remained for only seconds, but both saw her and the father, to have that one last remnant of memory, took the mirror away with him. However, over the years, it was discovered that any mirror used in that room might at any time reflect the girl who had gazed at her own reflection there in sad despair.

Another White Lady

Missouri Ghosts told of the legendary white lady of Marceline, whose appearances always meant disaster for trainmen. St. Joseph's white lady was not lethal, but was thoroughly disturbing. Her story took up more than a whole newspaper column in very small print.

This tale was related by a woman, then white haired, who had lived it as a girl of about twenty years. She had gone to a local mansion to keep a friend company while the friend's parents took a week-long trip. The house was centered in an acre of woods, but it did not occur to the guest to be afraid when she spent an afternoon alone there while her friend, Marie, made some calls. The guest, whom we'll call Jane, had a piece of needlework she wanted to finish and was enjoying the peace of the luxurious house. Somewhere not too close at hand a yard man was mowing grass and the cook would be coming in at any time to start the evening meal.

When Jane heard the back door latch raise, she assumed it was the cook, but was surprised that footsteps went upstairs, entered one of the bedrooms and did not come back down. Jane went to the stairs and called out to see if Marie had, for some reason, entered at the back door. Receiving no response, Jane said she was overcome with apprehension. What if a burglar was in the house? What was her duty as guest? She could only retreat into her own room and lock the door until Marie returned.

By the time her friend came back, however, Jane could not bring herself to relate such a trivial episode. But a day later, at about six o'clock in the evening, the sun still shining, Jane started upstairs for something she needed. As she reached the landing, she said "I suddenly stopped. I had heard no sound and felt no touch, but something stopped me. I can only describe it as shock like having a bucket of cold water poured over me."

There, in an open bedroom door, stood a handsome but as Jane described it "spectacularly tall," woman. The woman was dressed all in white, and over her long dark hair, which hung loose, was a white band that crossed the top of her head and fell down on each side of her face. The woman smiled sweetly and looked directly into Jane's eyes, and Jane began composing an explanation for being so startled and staring. There was nothing unnatural looking about the woman except her height but as their eyes held, Jane became certain that she was in the presence of something alien and dangerous. She felt, somehow, that it was essential for her not to show fear or revulsion, so she apologized for intruding and managed to make an unhurried departure.

Jane did, however, insist on going home for the night, so the girls traveled across town, and told about the incident. Jane's mother sent one of Jane's brothers back with them and arranged that each night one of the boys would sleep in Marie's home. Then something happened that solved the mystery.

While playing the piano one evening, Marie threw up her hands and screamed and both girls saw the white lady standing quietly in the big double doorway, looking not in the least threatening and not lingering long. The method of her departure was not described. Did she disappear or walk up the stairs? At any rate, Marie then explained.

Her mother had married a doctor whose deceased former wife had owned the house they lived in. When he moved his new family there, the former wife made herself obvious, but more in a reproachful than a threatening way. For instance, when the new wife and her sister returned from prayer meeting one evening, they saw the former lady of the house entering just before them. Merely seeing her in such ways seemed threatening, for the family members were always afraid something worse would happen. And then began such disturbances as inexplicable noises and beds rocking. The doctor and his new wife had discussed selling the house, but felt that doing so so quickly would raise questions and make the sale hard. They had hoped to wait a year or so longer.

When Marie's parents returned and heard what had happened, though, they sold the house at once, taking a severe loss. Apparently the white lady troubled the buyers, for they too sold the place quickly, and the third owner put it up for sale shortly after moving in.

Spending her last week in the neighborhood, the newspaper said, this last owner slept across the street at a friend's house and they looked out one night to see the haunted house ablaze with lights. These did not stay on long, but all knew the electrician had been there that day to disconnect everything.

When this happened again the following night they summoned the workman again and he showed them that lines connecting the house to the city power source were all detached. The next person to buy the house had it torn down and it was said that when demolition began all the bells in the house — apparently meaning those for calling servants — began to ring and jangle at the same time.

Some credit should be given, and some gratitude expressed to the St. Joseph reporter who collected the last two stories which were in a page of outstanding ghostly data from 60 or 70 years ago. Introductory material said this was a woman, but did not give her name.

Also Selected Short Subjects

The stories from St. Joseph are so numerous and some are so long and complex that the best treatment seems to be picking out bits that are most unusual or seem to give insights into another world.

A local woman mailed to the NP/G a report of a friend's hauntings. Thread, threaded through the several necessary slots, hooks and spools on a sewing machine, completely disappeared while she briefly used the telephone in another room. The family, together, repeatedly heard sounds from upstairs that seemed to be boxes falling and glass breaking, but when they went to look, nothing was ever out of order. One time a figure was seen in the hallway, through sheer curtains on French doors, but disappeared as they looked. When they went into the hall it was empty, doors all locked on the inside as the family had left them.

One family reported that almost nightly they saw a man's figure in coat and hat move past their picture window, seemingly walking very close to the house.

When they went out nobody was ever in sight up or down the street, and circling their house disclosed nobody and no sign anyone had been there.

🐦 A mother on Bon Ton Street reported that she never went upstairs alone in her house because she so strongly sensed a presence there and had once felt a touch on her shoulder. Her son, who slept upstairs, found only one disturbance — the recurrent sensation of something running over his body in bed, something heavier than any of the family's pets.

Final Word From a Psychic

Another Kansas City psychic, Betty Johnson, was quoted at great length in ghost-filled pages of the St. Joseph newspaper. While evaluating Nancy's home, apparently one of the most haunted in the city, she suggested something new to most of us as a reason why spirits choose not to go on into the hereafter.

"A lot of times," she said, "they think they're going to be judged." She listed some of the relatively minor sins that any of us might be concerned about if we faced heavenly court. "They are afraid that what waits them there might be worse than staying here bodiless."

Having herself been told that during childbirth she clinically died, Johnson feels that she has experienced something different than we expect. "There is a light available to spirits," she said, and described this as leading to a place that is neither heaven nor hell. It's a place where we meet loved ones who went before us and have the opportunity to learn from them about the afterworld before we have to enter it. "We've been taught to suppose we will go directly to heaven or to hell at the moment of death," she said, "but I don't believe that's the way it is."

This theory is interesting when compared to one set forth in a 1916 book named *Raymond or Life and Death*. It was written by Sir Oliver Lodge, a colleague of Arthur Conan Doyle's in exploring the unknown. Lodge lost his son in WWI and through various efforts to communicate with his spirit concluded that Raymond was telling him of a transitional period during which anything is available to a spirit that the body found necessary. This eases entrance into another way of life.

The recently departed, Raymond said, can live in houses exactly like those they loved on earth, can eat as long as that is important to them, can pursue their favorite recreations and work, all the while enjoying the company of loved ones who live on a different plane. Newly arrived spirits soon recognize more satisfactions than earth can offer and gradually come to prefer the lives their loved ones demonstrate to them. Once they are willing to give up all that had tied them to earthly life, they go with joy into a richer existence.

Haunted Houses

Chapter Nine

All the Usual

If a house was seated on some melancholy place, or built in some old romantic manner, or if any particular accident had happened in it, such as murder, sudden death or the like.... That house had a mark set on it, and was afterwards esteemed the habitation of a ghost.
Bournes' Antiquities.

Next to conventional white-clad or transparent ghosts, our favorite image of the unknown probably is summed up in the words "haunted house." We instantly visualize a deserted, decaying mansion, standing apart from its neighbors, a place whose very appearance is forbidding. We are certain that if we tried to approach it, we'd be impeded by an atmosphere thick with hostility. If we ventured inside, we know there'd be oppressive silence — at first. Then the door would slam behind us and when we ran to it, we'd find it locked and then...and then....

Maybe many stereotype haunted houses exist, but ghostly stories often have settings that are pleasant and busily occupied. For instance, St. Louis psychic investigator Bevy Jaegers was once called with her squad of counterparts to help a family living in an apparently haunted modern apartment. Residents on each side of this family reported no problems.

Our "First" House First

In 1998 a beautiful book about the Governor's Mansion was published in Jefferson City. Naturally, the house is believed to have some ghosts. How could it not, having stood so long and seen so much drama? In *If Walls Could Talk*, Missouri's First Lady Mrs. Jean Carnahan acknowledged this even as she assembled — in a scholarly way — hundreds of illustrations and the essence of uncountable state documents to tell the story of each governor's family preceding hers in this lovely 1871 house.

At Halloween time in 1997, television station KRCG in Jefferson City carried a series of ghost tales set in Central Missouri. One concerned a little girl encountered in the attic of the governor's mansion. As the story was related, cameras shifted to the lawn and a fountain ornamented by the bronze figure of a child happily dancing in the spray. The statue was said to have been cast in memory of that girl in the attic.

She is believed to be a nine-year-old named Carrie Crittenden, who died in 1883. Her father, Governor Thomas Crittenden, is remembered partly for taking a successful stand against bandit and guerrilla activity in the state and is credited for setting in motion events that resulted in Jesse James' death and Frank James' surrender.

During Crittenden's most stringent efforts, Mrs. Carnahan tells us, his life was threatened, as was the well-being of his daughter. Thereafter, he kept bodyguards with lively, golden-haired Carrie at all times. Like other powerful people of his era, though, he was helpless against disease. Diphtheria took Carrie just as it took thousands of other Missouri children. He expressed his grief in a song, "My Child," that he wrote and published after her death.

Mrs. Carnahan's book and other sources say that during Governor Christopher Bond's tenure, exactly 100 years after Carrie's death, a repairman came down from the attic at the end of a day's work and said to a member of Mrs. Bond's staff, "You might want to mention to them that their little girl is playing around up there. She spent most of the day with me."

When told that the Bonds had no little girl, he insisted, "Well, then it must be some neighbor's, because she hung around me for hours. She was eight years old or so, wearing a white dress."

A search of the attics and staircases disclosed no child. Some sources say that particular worker did not return to finish his project.

So far as is recorded, Carrie — first person to die in the current mansion — has not appeared since that day in the attic. Neither of the other two people who died in the mansion seems to have returned in ghostly form. One was Governor John Sappington Marmaduke, who served from 1885 to 1887. He'd been in the Confederate Army and reportedly told his fellow soldiers, camped across the river in view of the mansion, that he would someday live there. The other person who died in the mansion was Mrs. Alexander Dockery, the former Mary Elizabeth Bird. She had been a semi-invalid when she came to the mansion but still managed to be an active and admired first lady. Her death came on January 1, 1903. By interesting coincidence, each of these three people died during the holiday season and so lay in state among festive decorations.

According to KRCG, other haunts inhabit the mansion, but none seem connected to any particular event of its 129-year history. Objects do move around at times, the documentary said, and other inexplicable things happen. Candles put out fresh for some event are found shortly after, melted down from use. Sounds reported, mainly by guards who are in the mansion at night, are of quiet merriment, like guests assembling for one of the many fetes the mansion has seen. Sometimes barely audible voices and ripples of laughter seem to move up the stairs or through the hallways, as if groups were making their way to the ballroom or dining room.

Only once has anything alarming enough happened that a guard resigned. He was on duty alone, the book says, when the mansion's elevator began moving about erratically. He suspected vandals at once, and was alarmed at what this could mean for the building's priceless historic contents. Although he most likely called immediately for reinforcements, he also sprinted up and down stairs with drawn gun, trying to intercept the elevator. It remained unresponsive to calls, and continued to zip about, stopping here and there. No vandalism was found and no sign of forced entry, but it's easy to understand the guard's panic. No report exists of the elevator misbehaving since that night. Undoubtedly it was thoroughly examined and serviced to reassure everyone that it could be used again without fear. And undoubtedly, such an occurrence makes everyone in the mansion happy to accept unthreatening little mysteries like footsteps heard in carpeted areas where actual footfalls would be silent.

A Tricycle Ghost

Cal Dothage of Iron County speaks freely about an interesting little ghost who shared his life for several years. In 1970 he and a partner bought a two-story white farm house in the Arcadia Valley near Ironton and made a restaurant of it. Dothage says that in the five months it took to remodel the place, they noticed a number of unusual sounds in the house, but blamed them on winds that blew across the open fields surrounding them. In spring of 1971, when they opened their restaurant, which they called "Plain and Fancy," Dothage says "...the sounds took on a different tone, more like a person walking or playing in the front part of the house. These sounds never came past the front hall and front room and that's when we started to get the feeling that maybe more was going on than just the wind."

Dothage describes a sensation he once had of someone standing next to him in the hall when he knew nobody else was in the house. He mentioned this to nobody, not wanting to make his waitresses nervous, but a few weeks later one of them asked if he ever felt someone was in the hall. The next interesting experience came when he was in the kitchen and one of his waitresses was upstairs in the office. Cal heard his name called from the front hall and went to see what Carol wanted. She was coming down the stairs to see what he wanted, for she'd heard him calling her. With the similarity in names, he says, it's easy to see why both responded. But who had called them?

Dothage says he spent a little time after that trying to talk to whomever shared the house, but with no luck. He could now hear the sounds of a tricycle in the front rooms, "...one of those old-fashioned metal tricycles...you could hear rattling wheels and a tinkling of the bell as she rode around."

In years that followed, those sounds continued and various unusual things happened in the house. Only a few times, however, did employees or customers comment about feeling disturbed. One guest said she felt something against her in the hall and apologized, not realizing for a moment that nobody was there. Dothage comments that a psychic friend told him the reason there is often such strong disagreement about whether or not a place is haunted: some people are receivers while some are too busy transmitting into the present to feel anything from the spirit world.

But one night four people together saw the little cyclist. Dothage and three of his staff had closed the restaurant and were getting ready to leave, standing together in the back dining room with a direct view of the front porch. "We all saw the same thing at the same time," he says, "a small girl dressed in a yellow dress with a high collar." Some of the people with Dothage that night had heard him talk about his resident ghost and some had not.

"I went up to the porch," he says "but there was nothing there. This was the first time anyone had seen her, but it was not the last." The child made another appearance at Christmas time that same year. A friend, down from St. Louis for dinner, took a picture of the restaurant's Christmas tree. The next weekend he made another trip to show them what his film had captured.

"Looking in from the upper part of a window was the little girl in her yellow dress," Dothage says. "As this part of the window was eight feet above the ground, she had to be standing on air. Off and on for the rest of the time we owned the house, she made herself known in one way or another."

In 1978, *Missouri Life* magazine did a story on the restaurant, and among materials Dothage loaned them was that picture of the Christmas tree. After their article appeared, he received everything back — except that one picture. The friend in St. Louis was never able to locate the negative.

Dothage tried repeatedly to find out if the history of the house would shed any light, but it did not. He concluded that the child must have been from a different house on the same site, "That could be the reason she never came beyond the front rooms, and why she appeared to be standing on a floor higher than ours."

Whittemore House

According to Robbi Courtaway in *Spirits of St. Louis*, a lively seance at Whittemore House in May, 1972, was basis for the film *"Ghostbusters"*. Gordon Hoener, a St. Louis psychic investigator who participated in the event told her this. For the incident in question, readers can go to Courtaway's gripping book. Here's part of the underlying background as offered in a *St. Louis Post Dispatch* article on October 26, 1986.

Donated to Washington University by the heirs of the Whittemore family, the mansion was renovated at a cost of $550,000 to serve as a faculty club. The late Art Kleine was hired to manage the building in its new role. He told reporter Christine Bertelson that he began with a hearty disregard for ghost stories. His experiences in the house changed him and elicited this memorable statement: "If you believe in God, you believe in something supernatural. If you believe there is good, then it is possible that there is bad. I hate to say I believe in ghosts, but after the noises I have heard, the things I have seen...."

For some time, Kleine was able to dismiss the sounds he heard as natural to any house built at the turn of the century. But working there alone at night on bookkeeping, he grew more and more uneasy. "Things were hard to pin down," he told Bertelson, "but they happened so often I began to have an eerie feeling like I was not alone." Too frequently he had to interrupt his work to check doors and windows to make sure nobody could have entered the house. He changed his schedule so that he could do book work during daylight hours.

Manifestations intensified to the point that guests complained of sleep ruined by the sounds of doors and windows opening and closing. Kleine himself heard heavy footsteps in the unoccupied room just above his office and the atmosphere around him was at times oddly cold. Once he heard wire coat hangers in a meeting room closet jangling loudly and while he paused to listen, they jangled again.

Finally Kleine saw something, which he compared to a cloud of room deodorant spray, wavering and quick to disappear. This was not a one-time phenomenon, but he at least was spared the sight some kitchen employees reported, of a half a man — that is, just from the waist up — at the cutting board.

Kleine's own worst experience came after a large and successful reception. When he was closing up the building, he heard angry voices in the lobby, "like several men yelling," he says. When he went to look, of course, Kleine found nobody there and the front doors locked as he had left them after the last guest departed. When Kleine returned to his office, the sounds in the lobby began again and he said, "What I did then shows how sure I was that there were intruders in the house." He went to the kitchen and armed himself with the largest knife he could find. Nothing else happened and he was thankful his closing-up duties were almost done. He said he was never so happy to be back in his car and headed home.

At this point, Kleine reported events to college administration, but was told that there had to be a natural explanation for all he had witnessed and been told by employees and guests. He must not rock the boat, must not create publicity that would make the institution look silly. The story didn't say whether Kleine resigned or lost his job, but it did quote the manager who followed him.

She had seen and heard nothing herself, but the staff persisted in reporting the half-man and other strange things to her.

Near the end of the *Post Dispatch* story was a statement from Alberta Jackson, a housekeeper at Wittemore House. She said she often felt "something like a wind passing over my arm," but she was not frightened enough to resign her job. "I figure I never did anything to it, so why should it do something to me?"

Strange Doings in Republic

Joyce O'Neal, editor of *Senior Living* magazine, reported in that publication in October of 1997 on her family's experience living in a turn-of-the-century house in Republic, near Springfield. She said she and her husband bought the place in 1963, charmed by its "carpenter" style and its roominess. It had belonged to a hero of the Civil War and stood where his log cabin had once been. They knew that many families had lived in the house, that over the years it would have seen many deaths and other drama, but, she says, "We brushed aside the rumors that it was haunted."

They found, however, that their dog sometimes refused to go upstairs. Their children, who slept up there, often reported seeing gauzy figures moving about, sometimes standing near their beds. Once accustomed to this, the children said it was not frightening, but made them feel calm and peaceful.

O'Neal says she and her husband never saw anything, but did hear strange sounds including the crash mentioned in another chapter. And they did find something curious in remodeling. Behind what they thought was an outside wall was a tiny room occupied only by a large portrait of a man and woman, which raised disquieting questions. Since the picture was not removed before the wall was put up, it must have been the reason for building the wall. What could have happened to make people so determined to hide the picture forever, but unwilling to just take it down and dispose of it in some way? Of course, the picture could have been left as an oversight by someone who simply wanted to change the contour of the room. Inquiries in the area led the O'Neals to one person who thought the couple in the picture were distant relatives of hers but she had no idea why their picture had been isolated.

The O'Neal family saw many happy years in the house and added numerous features to enhance its beauty, indoors and out. One of their additions was a swimming pool. They gave special attention to atmospheric Halloween parties and none of these were visited audibly or visibly by any haunts. During the couple's tenancy, both their mothers died there, both at an age and in conditions of health that kept these deaths from being remarkable in any way. A former son-in-law killed himself in the back yard, but his emotional state had nothing to do with the house.

When the O'Neals sold the place, it was to a man who wanted it for a funeral home and remarked repeatedly on how perfect it would be for that purpose. Before he had completed the remodeling he planned, the house burned and he lost his life in the fire.

Our Oldest Haunted House

One of the oldest buildings in Missouri's oldest town, St. Genevieve, is the Guibourd House. Since 1939 its inhabitants have reported assorted hauntings. It would be interesting to know if there were others, earlier. The house was built in 1784, only 34 years after the first Creole families settled in an area that was to become part of the Louisiana purchase in 1803 and in 1812 become part of Missouri Territory. The builder, Jacques Dubreuil, was a native of France and his descendants occupied the house until 1906. Some of their tragedy could be blamed for the hauntings, perhaps. A daughter, Victorine, died under its roof while quite young and a son killed himself there.

The first record of unusual happenings was when Jules Valle, a new owner, recovering from surgery, claimed to feel a touch on his shoulder. Then he saw three little old men dressed in rough woolen shirts — but minus the lower halves of their bodies — beside his bed. Because they smiled and nodded, he concluded they had come to assure him of recovery and extended life. He did live for ten more years.

Valle's much younger wife, Anne-Marie, never saw those particular apparitions, but said she always felt presences in the house. After a favorite servant, Dora, died, Anne-Marie continued to hear the woman's familiar footfalls in the apartment she had occupied. Anne-Marie took this as a comforting message that Dora was not really gone and still cared about her. Other servants who came to the house told of hearing the footfalls too.

Nothing frightened Anne-Marie until a night when loud slamming sounds came from her late husband's bedroom, sounds suggesting heavy objects being thrown against the walls, and accompanied by glassy crashes and tinklings. Next morning when she gathered the courage to look, Anne-Marie expected to find a scene of destruction, but nothing was changed, nothing had been damaged. Suddenly outraged at the fear she had suffered the night before, Anne-Marie screamed to the poltergeists or whatever they were that they could never frighten her away from the house and might as well leave it themselves. As we find in so many poltergeist stories, the noise-makers seemed to take her seriously and disturbed her no more.

Anne-Marie reported numerous unusual happenings in the house. She said that one of her dogs frequently became frightened and cringed and hid, then desperately wanted to go outside. Another, Jamie, would focus on a spot, growl softly and barely wag his lowered tail as he did when meeting a new dog. She told of still another dog, Peter, who was especially fond of one of her friends. When this woman visited after Peter's death, Jamie did his greeting act several times, and they wondered if Peter had come to visit with his human friend.

All these accounts come from *Haunted America*, a 1994 book by Michael Norman and Beth Scott, authors of several collections of ghost stories. They said that when they visited Guibourd-Valle House, the then caretaker, Kristine Basler, told them of a few experiences that seemed related to the earlier haunts. She sometimes heard classical music being played on the piano that was present in the days of Victorine, a pianist. It sounded like diligent practice, with many repetitions. Her own record player's turntable at times spun so fast that it could not be used. Light bulbs sometimes flared and faded, sometimes went off and came on. Kristine described a frequent unnerving effect of something obscuring light temporarily, as though somebody had passed between her and the lamp.

Kristine said she felt uncomfortable in Jules' bedroom even in daylight when conducting tour groups through the house and would not have considered going there alone at night. Eventually, she moved her sleeping arrangements into what had been slave quarters at the rear of the house. Though she knew great physical suffering and emotional turmoil had to have existed there, Kristine said nothing ever disturbed her rest.

Huggable and Slightly Haunted

"I can identify with tree huggers," Elaine
Derendinger of Franklin told me long ago, "because I
sometimes hug my house." She was reacting then to
something I'd written about trees, but only now can I
react to what she said. After visiting her historic house
and interviewing her about its apparent, but very mild
hauntings, I asked her about the hugging. Just how does
one do this?

"On the east end," she told me, "when the sun has
warmed the bricks, I just spread my arms out and hug."
One can easily imagine that the warm bricks seem to
pulsate faintly, like a living creature. It would be easy to
fancy that the house was responding. And if ever a house
responded to love, this one should.

Elaine had loved it for years before she and her
husband, George, bought it. They used to drive by often,
admiring the building's lines, awed by the history it has
seen, sad that part of it was being used for hay storage.
There was almost no chance it would ever know respect-
ful, affectionate restoration; neglect, deterioration and
eventual razing is the fate of all too many wonderful old
houses.

Circumstances, however, combined to make it possible for the Derendingers to buy the place and its ten
acres. This was in 1964 and their restoration still is not
complete, for there was a great deal to do, most of it quite
expensive. Elaine says that without George's carpentry
skills, they could never have done what they've done.

History of Cedar Grove is given in *The Story of
Howard County*, which Elaine helped to write and
compile in 1999. Cedar Grove was built in 1824 by a
pioneer farmer named Nicholas Amick. What he chose
was Federal style and he reared eleven children there.

The second owner, Horace Kingsbury was a doctor and from various business undertakings became a wealthy man. He added a large Greek Revival section to the house. Elaine believes that her home may be the only one in Missouri to combine these two styles. Cedar Grove is listed in both the Missouri Historic Sites Catalog and the National Register of Historic Places. Among its notable features are fireplaces in every room, some 15-inch-thick walls and separated staircases to separated sections of the house.

One unforgettable feature of Cedar Hill is that the Santa Fe Trail runs only a few yards from the front door. Early residents of the house would have daily witnessed traffic on that revered route. And, across some cornfields, the Missouri River rolls, usually at a safe distance, but in floodtimes, a possible menace. Once Elaine saw it almost in her front yard and she says one of the eeriest experiences of her life was in the flood of 1993, listening as the familiar sound of rustling tall corn become counterpoint to rising water that gurgled and roared through it.

The hauntings: A Derendinger daughter, Chris, alone in the house, watched a rocking chair rock briskly in the next room. All members of the family witnessed, at one time or another, the bathroom door — in earlier times an exterior door — opening just a bit as they walked by, as if someone peeked out. And a visitor who came when the family was away and intended to wait for them left abruptly, made uncomfortable by "something."

The old house seems to have given its loving custodians many clues to the lives lived there previously. Elaine has found writings of Dr. Kingsbury and one of his textbooks as well as his saddlebags, full of antique bottles. Lying flat on a rafter, as if placed there for safekeeping, she found a blue violin-shaped bottle which she treasures so much that she always uses both hands to hold it.

Elaine says she has often wished she could go outside her house and look into the lighted interior while former residents go about their business. She'd particularly like to see one of the families gathered around a table to eat. Could it be that some of what we consider ghostly visitations stem from a reverse on this impulse? Maybe beings from the past just enjoy revisiting their old homes in what is to them the future?

There grows the hours' ladder to the sun
Each rung a love or losing to the last...
My father's ghost is climbing in the rain.
Dylan Thomas, *I Followed Sleep*

Chapter Ten

And Some
That Should Be

Some stories are so vague that a listener may feel "they're doing their best to have a ghost, but...." Some houses are so atmospheric or steeped in significant history or in tragedy that people say, "if it's not haunted, it should be!" From these sources may come stories as memorable as the most eerie of those about seemingly genuine haunts. Here are some examples.

The Gentle Spirit of Salem

"Dare to whisper about the bizarre incidents this Halloween. ...Myrtle, dressed in her sun-bonnet, tending to the flowers which grew so well for her...she was a sweet, gentle woman who deserves to be remembered."

This tribute, created by Renee J. Raper for the *Salem News* in October, 1990, concludes a story that also contains a description of Myrtle Henderson, found on August 27, 1963 in one of her outbuildings, wrapped in bed sheets and oilcloth, and sprinkled with quick lime, identifiable only by her wedding band.

Mrs. Henderson, highly respected by her neighbors, had lived for decades in an historic Dent County house.

Built in 1841 by David Henderson (no relation), the house saw the beginnings of Salem. Henderson gave the town its name.

In this house, Myrtle had lost one son as a small child and had reared at least one other, Vernon, who was living with her at the time of her death. He noted the event on October 19, 1962 by writing on the kitchen calendar "Sad Day". At first, naturally, Vernon was suspected of having killed his mother, who was in her 80s and in failing health. But the doctor, who had visited her in September and previously, said he never saw any trace of neglect or abuse and added that nothing in Myrtle's manner indicated that she feared Vernon. Neighbors said he kept the place clean and waited on his mother kindly.

All understood why he had impersonated Myrtle for almost a year, wearing her sunbonnet and long dresses to tend the flowers and go to the mailbox. They knew why he had continued having her prescriptions filled. He was afraid her death would be discovered and he'd have to go back to the penitentiary in Kansas. Because his mother needed his help, he'd been given an early release from a term earned by shooting and wounding his estranged wife. He'd been placed in Myrtle's custody, so it would have been to his advantage for her to live forever. This reasoning apparently prevented his being tried for murder. If Vernon returned to prison the story doesn't say so, and it doesn't say how his mother's body happened to be found. It's not surprising, of course, that people of the area considered the Henderson farm haunted.

Confederate Hill

Some rather wispy stories do exist about this lovely antebellum mansion, one of the few still left in Columbia, and listed on the National Register of Historic Places. It's said that from a distance only, grey-clad soldiers have been seen moving around the grounds, as have apparent slaves, going about their tasks. There is speculation that the builder, David Guitar, used cellars or tunnels under his home as hospital for Southern soldiers smuggled to him from engagements in Missouri.

However, to general knowledge, at least, no great tragedy took place at Confederate Hill. Rather, an exceptional act of brotherly love was demonstrated there. As the Civil War began to become reality, Odon Guitar wanted Missouri to remain neutral. When that proved impossible, he went with the Union, though his brother David's sympathy was passionately for the South. Both became officers, Odon a general in the Union forces. He distinguished himself by stopping Sterling Price's planned invasion of Missouri and so had influence. When Union forces were stationed in Boone County, he was able to give orders that his brother's house should not be touched.

Despite this, we're told, the two were estranged for the rest of their lives, not even speaking, though both lived in Columbia. David reared a family of ten in the house his brother had secured for him. Odon became an important community leader and served two terms in the state legislature.

Confederate Hill was most recently occupied and cared for as a home by Harvey and Miriam McCaleb. After four decades of residence, Mrs. McCaleb died near there in an automobile accident in 1997 when she was 86 years old. As this book was written, Confederate Hill and the 26 acres remaining from its original 862 were for sale again after a few years' respite from the possibility of being subdivided. Plans had not worked out to make it an "event site," a place where weddings, receptions, reunions, business conferences and such could be held.

Certainly Confederate Hill would have provided a beautiful setting, and the rumors of its being haunted would have enhanced it for many people.

Rivercene

Another beautiful Missouri house is 132 year old Rivercene, survivor of the great flood of 1993 and many lesser ones. Try as they will, people cannot find anything unearthly about this mansion at New Franklin, across from Boonville, except to say that it has a definite aura of other times and other worlds. Some feel its flood survivals are a bit uncanny.

Rivercene was built in 1864-69 by a riverboat captain named Joseph Kinney who wanted to be able to step ashore from his boat to his home. He declared that the river would never enter its ground floor. Kinney had lived through the flood of 1844, when the Missouri River crested at 33 feet. He reasoned that such an extreme event was hardly likely to be surpassed, so built Rivercene accordingly. The '93 flood crested at 37.1 feet and put a great deal of muddy water into Rivercene. Though considerable cosmetic damage resulted, the building stood firm, a tribute to its creators.

Rivercene almost acquired a ghost that summer, when Wayne Lammers, a Boonville man much attached to the house, spent more than eight hours in a nearby tree while flood waters roared past him at 35 miles per hour. He had come out to videotape the flood and wanted to see how Rivercene fared because he had helped with earlier renovations.

Due to a mishap with his boat, Lammers found himself and his camera afloat. He took refuge in a tree where he waited for rescue. Lammers said that even under those circumstances — standing in water up to its downstairs windows and nobody knowing how much higher the flood might go — Rivercene was serenely beautiful. National television later aired his film and other footage made by Rivercene's present owners, Ron and Jody Lenz.

The nearest thing to a ghost story told about Rivercene is that there was a time when thousands of flies unaccountably hatched in one of its upstairs rooms, while none were seen elsewhere in the house.

The Baker House

In Montgomery county near Danville stands a house that is almost unchanged from the way it looked during the Civil War.

The history of this place should give rise to a spirit or two. The infamous "Bloody Bill" Anderson was said to have visited there, so to dramatize the house on special occasions, a reenactor rides a horse through the straight front-to-back hall.

This is something Southern cavalrymen seemed prone to do, either as ultimate insult to enemies or as a way of legally greeting their own families when fighting brought them near home but they were not supposed to leave their unit. A man could honestly say that he never got off his horse even though he had visited his parents or wife and perhaps received some home-cooked food to take away with him.

Stories about the Baker House involve threats and attempts to burn it, and one story mentions a mounted soldier snatching up an infant or small child, and simulating carrying it off, but leaving it safely in the yard..

Owners Mary Ann and Noel Crowson have nothing unusual to tell about the house from their own experience, but during restoration, a workman told them that while eating his lunch in the yard, he looked up and saw a woman watching him from an upstairs window. He went in to tell her it was unsafe to be in the house while construction was going on, but he could find nobody. He afterwards refused to be in the house alone.

Mrs. Crowson's research gives some validation to the idea that a family member could have been stationed in an upstairs window to watch for intruders in the post-war era of lawlessness. The matriarch of the family had her bed brought downstairs and situated so she could see both front and back doors.

The episode starring Anderson seems to have gone more or less like this: he brought his guerrilla band to the Baker House hoping to kill its owner, a Union supporter. Baker was not there, so the outlaws contented themselves with trashing the women's bedrooms and possessions ("symbolic rape," Mrs. Crowson says) and setting fire to Mrs. Baker's mattress.

Soon after they rode out, one young man returned alone and put out the fire. He's said to have first carried an infant into the yard and put it down at a safe distance from the smoke-filled house. Mrs. Crowson speculates that the boy belonged to a local family that had benefitted from the kindness of Mr. Baker, reputed to have been a generous person who helped many people in his neighborhood. In any case, if the story is true, it means that one young man's following his better impulses spared a house that today is historic.

Mrs. Carmen Harvey of Montgomery City, relates a strange little experience in the Baker House. During a tour with Mrs. Crowson, while they had paused in one of the bedrooms, both heard an odd, fairly loud squeaking. Mrs. Harvey said she felt drawn to a mirror sitting on a rotatable stand on a dresser. When she moved the mirror slightly, both heard the squeaking sound again. The mirror was much too heavy to have been moved by a current of air caused by the opening of a door somewhere else. The floor was too solid for their footfalls to have caused vibration in the furniture the mirror stood on.

"She told me 'it's never happened before,'" Mrs. Harvey said "And she's taken many, many people through the house on tours."

The Baker House is open to the public; 573-564-5240 and 573-564-1000 are the numbers to call about schedules.

If there are ghosts on the Titanic, then this is surely how they move — floating through the corridors, no longer subject to the intense pressure or cold. What do they make of these strange creatures invading their elegant tomb?

Edward W. Marsh, James Cameron's *Titanic*, Harpers, 1997

Looking
Back

No one has ever come back from the other world. I can't console you, but one thing I can tell you, as long as my ideas are alive, I will be alive.

Albert Schweitzer, *Reverence for Life*

My previous book, *Missouri Ghosts*, contains several stories that need to be revisited. For some, readers sent additional interesting data. For others, significant sources of enhancing detail were discovered. In one instance, descendants pointed out serious error. The latter applies to the story of Haden House, a lovely Boone County farm home that had served as a distinguished restaurant, but was empty at the time I wrote of it.

Chapter Eleven

The
Haden Saga

The story in a nutshell: Haden House was built by
Joel Harris Haden, a young man who came to Missouri
from Kentucky in 1828 and in only a few years had
established himself as a successful farmer and businessman. One Haden House resident of the 1980s reported
two sightings of the apparition of a young woman.
People who worked in the restaurant also reported
various strange occurrences, none of them frightening.

Since Haden's young wife had died in the house, it
was assumed that the ghost was hers and that it was a sad
little spirit. Sources that had been accepted for many
decades as being accurate indicated that the young wife
was from another state, came here very young and
became ill rather soon, possibly from tuberculosis, possibly just from homesickness and general discontent.
They said nothing about her having a child.

The fact is that the young first wife was a Boone
Countian and produced all Joel Harris Haden's heirs by
way of her one offspring before dying, a daughter. This
girl grew up to marry locally and have several children,
most of whom were girls who married into families from

Boone County or nearby. Thus, there are, in the area, many descendants of Joel Harris Haden, though not many who carry on the family name.

After his first wife's death Haden married twice more and one of these women gave him two sons, but each boy died in early childhood. If tragedy engenders haunting, then these events would underline the possibility of spirits at Haden House. The first wife had to forfeit a lifetime in her beautiful home and leave her baby behind; the second wife lost her sons and, no doubt, her own life there. Haden probably died in the house and possibly his third wife and his mother also spent their last days under its roof.

An important correction: Joel Haden became one of Boone County's most prominent citizens. He was among those who pledged large sums of money to bring the University to Missouri to Columbia. He also built a number of impressive business places. Some of these are still in use. One of the less fortunate, lost to fire, was the city's first opera house, for years a welcome part of the area's cultural climate.

These facts increase the drama of Haden House. Earlier inaccuracies were pointed out by Darrell Haden, a Missourian now living in Tennessee, whose experience in that state provides this book with its best and most authentic ghost story (see chapter 15). Joel D. Haden of Columbia kindly loaned me his copy of the family history, so the truth about Haden House could be told.

Chapter Twelve

The
Lemp Mansion

What *Missouri Ghosts* relayed about this historic St. Louis place, now a restaurant/bed and breakfast, was only a fraction of its story. Sources originally reviewed included the book, *Lemp: The Haunting History* and many extensive newspaper and magazine articles about this family of brewers whose operations covered eleven city blocks and whose wealth was a phenomenon of their era. Added details have come from interviews, recent books about the ghostly and from Troy Taylor, editor of *Ghosts of the Prairie* magazine, who has written at great length about the Lemps. During his research, he spent a night in their former home.

Background: two generations of the Lemp family occupied the lavish home at 3322 de Menil and three men from two generations of the family killed themselves there. The mother of the family met a difficult death there at only 47, and a daughter died by her own hand in another home nearby. Still another family member died an untimely death, either in the brewery or, some say, in another state where he had gone hoping to recover his health.

The Lemp house saw at least one promising marriage destruct wretchedly and go into prolonged and scandalous court proceedings. It also saw the family fortune reduced to almost nothing because of The Great Depression. The house saw its family become nearly extinct, with hardly an heir and none named Lemp. From being one of the city's showplaces, the Lemp Mansion declined to conversion into apartments and finally to near flop-house status.

The vision and enterprise of a family named Pointer brought the house back to its former beauty and put it to a use that enables countless people to experience the architecture, decoration and furnishings of another time in history. During restoration, a great many strange things were observed in the house, including poltergeist-like movements and sounds. Apparitions were also reported.

A sample of the newer stories: a woman told me of someone she knew who was eating at the mansion with a group, keeping one hand in his lap as etiquette demands. When he raised his hand at the end of the meal, it was smeared with butter, though he had felt nothing at all.

One of the best Lemp stories came at a St. Louis signing of *Missouri Ghosts*. A docent at the house, where tours are a standard attraction, knows a woman who did — or perhaps still does — bookkeeping for the restaurant. This lady, whom we'll call Mrs. Carter, often worked when the house was closed to customers, so she'd have no distractions. Sometimes she was able to do her work in daytime, but sometimes it had to be at night.

One evening during the holiday season, some years ago, she was pleased to see the colored lights coming on as she drove in. That meant she'd not be entirely alone in the house, always desirable considering its reputation, and it meant whoever was there had noted her approach and was giving her a friendly, festive welcome. Inside the house, however, she could locate nobody and thinking the lights must have come on by a wiring miscue which could be dangerous, she turned them off. When they came right back on, the bookkeeper's feelings were divided between fear for the house and uneasiness for herself. Unable to dismiss her anxiety, she turned off the lights again and hurried to her office upstairs to get the documents and ledgers she would have used that night. She would work with them safely at home! Downstairs again, Mrs. Carter disconnected the lights — which had once more come on — and carefully locked doors as she always did. No doubt she was much relieved to be in her car. But as she drove away, Mrs. Carter glanced back and saw a disquieting sight. The colored Christmas lights were on again and as she watched, light flared in her office window. The understated nature of this story never fails to evoke shivers from listeners who hear it told aloud.

A persistent rumor about the Lemps has been pointed out for this book by several people. It refers to a belief in the neighborhood that the Lemp family included a child who was in some way afflicted and was kept in an attic apartment. The idea of a hidden relative was a common factor in many romances and mysteries of the 1800s, so one tends to give it very little credence in this case. But storytellers repeat that people reported seeing a "monkey-like" face in the attic windows and they speculate that the final suicide in the house was related to this person. Maybe, they say, Charles A. Lemp, who shot himself and his dog in the basement of the house in 1949, had been custodian for this secret family member. Perhaps when that person's death ended Charles' responsibility, he made his own escape from a lonely and burdensome life.

For more about the Lemps, read *Spirits of St. Louis* by Robbi Courtaway or the Lemp book by Stephen P. Walker, or ask Taylor (1-888-GHOSTLY) for a photocopy of his article.

Chapter Thirteen

The Exorcism

Missouri Ghosts' account of the following event didn't quote any of the priests involved or deal with the lingering question of whether the exorcism left behind troubled spirits that could be dangerous. Material found since then was mainly stories in St. Louis and Kansas City newspapers which revived the story for Halloween in the past several years. These stories help us to put a neat cap on the story.

But first, a refresher on what took place, with new data inserted: The boy affected was named Douglas Deen and he lived with his parents in a Washington D. C. suburb. His family felt that their problems began when he tried to reach a deceased aunt via Ouija board. The first manifestations were minor poltergeist-like sounds and actions which progressed to more serious things such as bloody scratches on Douglas' body and trancelike states in which he spoke in voices that seemed impossible for a small young boy, using language from other historical eras. At night Douglas grew so violent that his family sought help from assorted health professionals and religious sources.

When all seemed to fail, they were advised to try St. Louis University Hospital, operated by the Society of Jesus, an order of priests that still has rituals for exorcising demons. There a team worked for three months with

Douglas, their method being mainly to spend nights with him in constant prayer and with admonitions to the demons thought to inhabit him. The priests finally succeeded and Douglas went home and on to a normal life, which he lived in anonymity.

Though some of what the boy did while in the apparent power of demons was as repulsive as events depicted *"The Exorcist"* novel and movie based on this episode, nobody involved died then. All lived out normal lifespans. One of the senior priests, Father William S. Bowdern, was said by a *Post Dispatch* writer to have been permanently damaged physically and emotionally. Most of the men who worked with Douglas are gone now, but two priests quoted were scholastics (priests in training) at the time and had tasks as assistants to the others. Fathers Walter Halloran and Paul Reinert both told reporters that Douglas truly was possessed. Father Bowdern was quoted as saying the same to friends, though he never publicly discussed his role in the exorcism.

One loose end about Missouri's exorcism has been whether or not the rooms where it took place are haunted. Various stories have been told about them. The most prevalent has been that the rooms that saw this remarkable activity were sealed off, furniture inside, but still are the sites of strange happenings.

Actually, the *Post Dispatch* story said, Douglas was kept in the west wing of the old Alexian Brothers Hospital, long since razed. The house the Deen family occupied when their problems started has since burned. The reporter quoted some who said it was deliberately ignited by fire fighters to use for practicing their skills. He acknowledged that some sources called the fire mysterious. Perhaps a few loose ends still remain in the story of the exorcism.

Chapter Fourteen

Jim the Wonder Dog

No new revelations about this puzzling animal have surfaced since *Missouri Ghosts* reviewed his remarkable record, though a recent intriguing question has risen about him. But Jim was much in Missouri news on May 1, 1999, when his hometown of Marshall opened a park in his memory.

Jim was a Lewellyn setter who belonged to a Marshall couple, Mr. and Mrs. Sam Van Arsdale. Though as a puppy he did not at all meet standards of appearance and performance for his breed, his owners soon realized they had something incredible in their house. They had no doubt that Jim understood most of what they said to him and a great deal that was not put into words. He not only became unbelievable as a hunting dog, he did such uncanny things as these: go on request to the closest person to him who was wearing blue; go to the person who had two chows at home; go to the person who had never visited Marshall before.

Later Van Arsdale found that Jim could go out in the street and locate any given car when shown its license plate numbers written on a card, or told its make and color. Then Jim progressed to predictions. He could

choose from numbered cards the sex and number of
unborn babies, the outcome of World Series ball games
and national elections. He responded to questions in any
language or in shorthand or Morse code. And Jim
demonstrated ability to do such things whether or not his
owner was present. There seems to be no way that training or silent cues could have been employed.

Missouri Ghosts can take no credit for what has happened with Jim since 1997; the town of Marshall was
looking for ways to put itself on the map as part of a state
program to make Missouri more attractive to tourists.
That's why they built Jim's park, beautified with flowers,
a fountain and a bronze statue of him. Adjacent is a small
museum of Jim memorabilia. Already many thousands of
visitors have found the park and as a result, Jim has been
featured widely over the US and beyond, in newspapers
and magazines, on radio and television and online. At
least one movie is being prepared on his life.

Missouri Ghosts presented Jim only as one of our
state's four unexplainable phenomena, but now the whole
world is becoming aware of him and will be sharing the
questions some Missourians have long pondered: what
did Jim's abilities mean? Could we have found out more
from this dog about the hereafter and the purposes of our
lives if we had known how to ask him?

One Marshall resident who knew the Van Arsdales
said she would not be surprised to know the couple had
been able to question Jim on such subjects, using "yes"
and "no" cards. She also feels sure they'd never have told
what they learned because of attitudes then about the
paranormal. As it was, some ministers called Jim a tool
of the devil and Van Arsdale a sinner for fostering him.
How would they have reacted to being told he had some
secrets of eternity to share?

But now for the new question about Jim:

Evelyn Counts is a Marshall resident who took a leading role in securing funds for Jim's park and making arrangements to bring the park into being. She traveled widely to give speeches and wrote a booklet about the dog for use in promoting his park and museum. Though Jim was dead before she and her husband moved to Marshall, Mrs. Counts undertook the job of immortalizing him because her late husband had been so captivated by the dog's exploits. As a traveling sales representative, Counts was regularly in Marshall and stayed at the Ruff hotel because that was where the Van Arsdales and Jim lived. Counts told his wife how unbelievable the dog was and how awe-struck his audiences always were.

One night in fall of 1999, when Mrs. Counts and a friend were closing up the park for the evening and locking its gate, they discovered a dog outside who stunned them.

"He was the very image of Jim," she says, "and he was behaving in a strange way. When we first saw him, he was staring at Jim's statue as if entranced. He would occasionally move away and then come back and stare some more."

She says that she wanted this dog from the moment she saw him. "It was as if it was meant to be," she says, though it has been years since she kept a dog of any kind and those she had were usually small. "If he's a stray, I want him," she told her friend. The other woman went to check for collar and tags. Though the Jim double wore none, he was well-groomed and in good flesh. He pleasantly accepted handling from a stranger, but made no effort to ingratiate himself. He went back to staring at the statue.

Then a pick-up truck passed and the Jim look-alike followed it for a little more than a block. The women supposed that the driver was his owner, that the dog lived on a nearby farm and had come to town in the truck. But

he did not follow with any great determination nor with the desperation one would expect from a dog who was being left behind. Instead of coming back to the women, the animal turned off on a street near them. They got in the car and drove down that street, but could not find him. "We couldn't imagine where he'd disappeared to so quickly," Mrs. Counts says now. "It was a business street with closed-up stores and empty parking lots and few cars out. We regretted very much that when my friend had hold of him we didn't just put him in our car. But he seemed like he had to be somebody's dog."

Next day and often since, Mrs. Counts has checked with Marshall's animal shelter and veterinarians. Nobody has seen a dog who looks like Jim and nobody knows of one in the area. Mrs. Counts can't believe that if there were one, the owner would not have come forward when her committee publicized its hope of finding a Jim replica for opening day pageantry at the park. She can't believe that such a dog could live in the town or nearby and nobody would be aware and mention it to others.

"I know that to many people I would sound nuts," she says, "but I can't really describe the feeling I had when I saw him. It was eerie, and if he turns up again and there is any way I can have him, I still want him."

There could be a perfectly sensible explanation, of course. The dog could indeed have come into town in the truck bed without his owner noticing that he was there, or with the owner's knowledge but without his later noticing "Jim's" departure. Maybe when the owner got home and discovered the absence, he drove back to town and cruised around honking his horn, drawing the dog to him immediately. There are those among us who would prefer to believe that the spirit of the original Jim made a brief visit from the other side to thank those who most honor his memory!

Chapter Fifteen

Deadman's Pond

Missouri Ghosts dealt briefly with a body of water in Stone County that figures in many anthologies of ghost stories. The most popular tale is about a young man who took his sweetheart to a dance, providing a horse for her to ride. After delivering her to her home, riding along leading the extra horse, the young man became aware, near the dreaded pond, that the animal was lagging. When he turned around it was to see, for a few seconds, a male rider on the horse. Other stories were about figures appearing and disappearing at the pond amidst cries, moans and shouts.

Apparently human skulls and bones actually had been found in the pond and people who live in the area tell me tradition says that these belonged to bandits or their victims, or to soldiers defeated in the area. However, Ina Cutbirth of Reeds Spring sent me a paper written for college by a young man she knew, John D. Harris. His prepared the paper in summer of 1975. It documents historical facts pertaining to the pond, facts far more interesting that the ghostly legends.

Harris wrote that Stone County was new at the time of the Civil War, having been organized only in 1851. Whatever protective agencies it had begun to develop for its citizens were depleted by members going to the military and Stone County's border position made it especially vulnerable to what Harris termed "the lawless elements spawned by the war." Outlaws, bushwhackers and escaped prisoners from both sides all rustled Stone County cattle and horses and raided farms and burned homes, killing anyone who resisted them.

Stone Countians organized a home guard to try to cope with these problems and Harris does not repeat what other writers have said about such groups, that they were, by necessity, composed mainly of boys in their early teens, aging men and perhaps some veterans discharged with disabilities. Their horses could not have been the best since intruders had so often combed the area for good animals. The guard surely had to make do mainly with plow and buggy horses. However, Harris comments that Stone County must have somehow preserved some of its assets, because Lucile Morris Upton, in her book, *Bald Knobbers*, referred to the Stone County guard as strong.

When the county was invaded by two groups of guerrillas, totalling about 120 men, the guard could not mobilize immediately because getting the word to members in their widely separated homes took a little time. Before the guard was assembled, the invaders had stolen 150 cattle and what few valuables the citizens of Galena still had. The brigands had camped at what would become Deadman's Pond on their first night in the area and planned to rendezvous there with their loot.

The guard did manage to ambush them on the old Wilderness Road between Reeds Spring and Galena. Using their small supply of ammunition carefully, they were able to pick off enough of the marauders that the others took flight, leaving most of the cattle behind. Assuming that the guard had done all it could do, the bandits made a leisurely camp at the pond. But just before dawn, they were surprised by the guard, which had surrounded them with a miraculously-obtained new supply of ammunition. Harris quoted Walter B. Stevens, author of a 1915 book called *Missouri, the Center State.* Stevens said that of the 120 men who invaded Stone County, only 20 escaped. If this is true, the carnage at the pond would have been a terrible sight and the disposal of bodies a formidable task.

So perhaps there is some validation here for the legend that says so many bodies were thrown into Deadman's Pond that for years its water was too rank even for cattle and wildlife to drink. For decades people claimed to have raked bones and skulls from the pond, according to Harris and other writers. Some of these were displayed there, so it's no wonder the place was avoided and people were more than ready to see ghosts.

> *To them, we're ghosts.*
> James Van Praage

Ghosts From Off

Where do we draw the line on what is and isn't a Missouri ghost? Must it have been seen within the boundaries of the state, or does any ghost seen or felt or sought anywhere by a Missourian qualify? What about remarkable stories heard by Missourians elsewhere and retold at home with great effect? Obviously we must find a stopping point before we include any ghost story heard of anywhere by any Missourian. But here are a few with strong state connections that are too good to ignore.

Chapter Sixteen

The Very Haunted Crescent

We are so advanced in our knowledge that we can prove the impossibility of ghosts?
Gotthold Ephriam Lessing, Hamburgische Dramaturgie

"If I'd known which rooms are haunted, I'd have insisted on having one of them," a Missouri friend said, after visiting the Crescent Hotel in Eureka Springs, Arkansas. Others have said "Oh, there's definitely an atmosphere there...downright creepy in places" and "The vibes are unmistakable." One Missourian told me that in an area she later learned had been the site of garden parties, she had "a sensation...this was not a vision...I didn't actually see or hear anything. They have a lot of gorgeous gardens there and I was sitting in one, my eyes closed, just absorbing the sun and the flower scents and bird songs. Gradually I began to feel that I was among women in light-colored, floaty summer dresses and that teacups were clicking lightly and music was playing."

Past owners of the Crescent have soft-pedaled such reports, fearing they would scare off customers, but present operators realize that many guests seek the place

out hoping to witness something mysterious. Here are
some of the apparitions and other manifestations that
have been reported at the Crescent.

꧁ A man in formal attire of the early 1900s comes
down the staircase, looks around as if meeting
someone, then takes up a position by the imposing
free-standing fireplace that dominates the lobby.
Carroll Heath, one of three partners who offer ghost
tours of the Crescent, says that employees believe
this is Dr. John Ellis, who was at one time staff
physician for the hotel. Some say they've seen him
leave the elevator and walk across the hall to the
small room he used as office. If the door happens to
be closed, he just walks through it. An aroma of fine
pipe tobacco often accompanies the doctor's appearances.

꧁ In the basement, which served as morgue when the
hotel was a hospital, a woman in what appears to be
a vintage nurses' uniform passes by. She is urgently
pushing an old-fashioned gurney and some
observers say it rattles as she goes.

꧁ An insubstantial, hard-to-define figure enters a
certain room through its closed door. Nobody seems
to have described what it does there, but at least one
couple who saw it packed immediately and checked
out of the Crescent in the wee hours.

꧁ On the staircase a young woman in gym clothes of
long ago — dark bloomers and a sailor style
overblouse — has been seen sometimes going up,
sometimes going down.

🐿 One person wrote of seeing a woman topple from a balcony and of watching her upturned face as she descended, mouth open in a scream, but without sound. He ran downstairs, expecting to find a crumpled body, but saw nothing. "There was something strange about the way she went off," he said. "I think she was pushed, but I saw nobody else."

🐿 Staff members working to prepare the Crescent for opening its season in other years said they several times heard, from the empty dining room, the sounds of conversation, laughter and dishes. After repeatedly looking and seeing nothing, they dismissed the sound as another of the Crescent's quirks and stopped even talking about it. Then one day a newcomer looked in and called others to witness the sight of an occupied table and a waiter serving desserts from a trolley.

🐿 Employees have reported hearing voices in various parts of the building when the hotel was closed. They have sometimes found problems with doors that cannot be opened if the employee is alone. These yield readily if another person — particularly a supervisor — is called to help or to see the phenomenon. Guests have sometimes asked the meaning of bells they heard ringing in different sequences. A leftover from days when the Crescent housed a women's college?

🐿 Morris, the hotel's late resident cat, who no doubt haunted the basement in life, seeking mice, still is reportedly seen there from time to time. He has the convenient ability now, however, of fading into the walls or marching sedately out of them. Possibly

Morris has the age-old excuse for ghost walking — disturbance of his grave. He was buried in one of two adjacent flower beds and a nice marker erected for him. A new gardener, however, thought it would be better if the beds were identical. He moved the marker and set up a mock burial site elsewhere.

A young former hotel employee who related some of these stories for Phillip Steele's videos about Ozarks ghosts said also that Morris had a major adventure in the haunted dining room. One night, while security people sat visiting during their break, Morris became very interested in the closed dining room door and gave his usual body language requests that it be opened for him. When it was, he went scampering in, and could be heard for about half an hour, tearing around, bouncing off walls and furniture, occasionally knocking something over as cats do when engaged in rowdy solo make believe, or games with another cat or possibly torturing prey. But what prey and what game would last so long?

The story teller said, "We were afraid to look." But when they opened the door, Morris emerged, with the satisfied mein of a cat who has had a very good time indeed. The observers looked carefully for another cat or for remains of successful predation and found nothing.

The history of the Crescent offers hints that might relate to some of these foregoing events. A young stonecutter named Michael died in a fall from high on the building while it was in construction, and recently he's been blamed for poltergeist action that will be described later. In the period of the Crescent's college era, a student is said to have either fallen or leaped from a balcony. While the building served as a hospital, some deaths undoubtedly occurred within its walls. Considering how many people have worked and lived in the Crescent, it must be saturated with human emotion of all kinds.

The hotel was built in 1884-86 at a cost of about a quarter of a million dollars, an investment of a company of businessmen. Spas were becoming more and more popular then and "the waters" of Eureka's 63 springs were considered particularly beneficial. The men reasoned correctly that a large, year-round luxury hotel would boost the economy of the whole area. Serving the hundred-room hotel created uncountable new jobs and business opportunities for Eureka Springs and the surrounding area. Constructed of white limestone native to the area, put together without mortar, the hotel stands, commanding and spectacular, on a hill overlooking the city. Each of its five stories has a wide balcony in front that adds to its palatial appeal.

The Crescent offered guests the latest in late 1800s luxury: steam heat, electricity in all rooms, private baths for most, elevators, beautiful views on every side. Entertainments available included tea dances every day, formal dances at night, horseback riding, boating, tennis, talley-ho rides (talley-hos were big vehicles holding large numbers of passengers and pulled by matched teams of four, six or eight horses).

The hotel bloomed until 1908 when declining patronage inspired the founding of a long-contemplated Crescent College and Conservatory for Young Women. For about two decades the select, expensive school prospered. Fully accredited, it assembled a faculty so respected that they drew students from 39 states. For part of that period, the Crescent operated as a hotel from late spring to early fall and as college for the other months. Then, affected by the Great Depression, the college closed. The hotel, with difficulty, maintained seasonal operation, but only for awhile.

The next owner of the Crescent was Norman Baker, an Iowa entrepreneur of questionable standards who made the hotel a hospital. He advertised processes of healing cancer "without surgery, radiation or X-ray." He redecorated the Crescent in a disturbing color scheme of purple and lavender, and thrived there from 1937 into 1940. Then, convicted of using the mails to defraud, he was put out of business and for several years the hotel stood vacant.

After World War II, the Crescent was extensively renovated and was restored to full-time hotel use. Since then it has been in continuous operation and continuous improvement. The hotel now offers 68 rooms including penthouse accommodations in picturesque cupolas.

And the restored Crescent has some new ghost stories. Several stories star Michael, the stonemason mentioned earlier. Supposedly he approaches people, identifies himself and offers help. Michael Norman and Beth Scott in *Haunted America*, described him as the typical handsomely blond and well-built Scandinavian and say his ghost cannot be distinguished from a living person. In life he fell to his death through several unfloored rooms. Carroll Heath says this fall was from the fourth floor to the basement, and that the space he fell through included the rooms that now are haunted. There, guests and employees have reported assorted poltergeist-like activities, including water and lights that go on and off of their own volition and doors that may be hard to open.

Heath says that he and his partners, some of whom are trained in clairvoyance as he is, spent considerable time in one of these rooms, trying different methods of reaching Michael. They got nothing at all, but when ready to leave, they could not open the door. Eventually, with combined force they did get it open and when they closed it, were treated to powerful noise and impact as if a gigantic Michael had kicked it from inside.

One summer day of 1999, at about 5 a.m., a female guest reported awakening to find a man bending over her, staring at her intently. He had dark hair and moustache and wore a high-collared Victorian looking shirt. Frightened, she roused her husband, but before he could share the experience, the intruder dematerialized before her eyes. The couple, though they promised to meet with the Ghost Tour team, left without doing so.

Numerous mystifying little things have happened at the Crescent, such as guests taking pictures and then finding on the prints someone who was not in their party. But the most colorful story features a Christmas tree. Heath says that not many years ago, the dining room was decorated with a lovely large tree in the corner, surrounded by beautifully wrapped fake gifts. One morning the staff found the tree in the opposite corner and all the packages ripped open. Tables and chairs had been placed in a semi-circle before the tree, as if for an audience. Michael? Heath said there seemed no possibility of this being a prank, because the dining room was closed and locked and the night watchman, only employee in the building that night, was a person totally beyond suspicion.

Chapter Seventeen

Southern Horses

This story began as a short entry in the archives of a Southern family, loaned to me by a friend for research apart from this book. If any ghost story ever aroused questions and invited expansion and enhancements, this one does. But the friend just shook her head in a rather embarrassed way and said, "Oh, I don't think that ever happened, at least not to my family. I think it's just an old tale." A few years later, at a book signing in St. Louis, a man told me he had the granddaddy of all ghost stories to share. He heard it, he said, while living in the south and thought it was just a traditional yarn, maybe based on truth, but gussied up considerably. Here's the essence of the two versions of that story, combined.

One December afternoon a young mother and her mother-in-law set out for a circle of visits to show off the newest member of the family, an infant only a few months old. They rode in a substantial closed vehicle that befitted their wealth, pulled by a magnificent team of four geldings of the owner's own breeding, a source of great pride to him. The driver, Charles, was a mature man of high ability, to whom the family would have entrusted anything. He had been with them for his lifetime and had trained all their most important horses, as well as this widely envied carriage team. Charles made a strikingly dignified picture in his livery, with an identically clad young grandson along to open doors, set up steps and do anything else necessary to make passengers comfortable.

Heading home after their day of satisfying socializing, the coach full of baby gifts, the mother and daughter were happily chatting, not apprehensive about the growing dark because their coach had lights and with Charles at the lines safety could be taken for granted.

They had just entered a canebrake on their own property, a place where high vegetation hastened darkness, when Charles shouted to them in a most uncharacteristic way. "Ladies!" he called, panic in his voice, "Shutter your windows! There's something after the horses!"

Immediately began a terrifying chorus of loud snarlings and roarings that seemed to come from huge-chested creatures unlike anything the ladies had ever heard of. The horses were screaming in terror and pain and Charles was shouting, his grandson wailing. Hearing the whip cracking viciously was a new sound to the ladies, almost as frightening as any aspect of their situation. Charles always drove by gentle voice; he never hit horses. If he had lost control, what might happen to them all?

The nightmare of noise and wildly rocking coach went on for a mile or more, until they started up the steep drive to their house. Here Charles always stopped as he did at any hill, so his grandson could release the check reins that held the horses' necks in a tight arch for the required fashionable silhouette. If they cannot lower their heads for uphill pulls, horses' breathing is painfully impeded and they can be badly damaged. Charles also ordinarily drove the last few miles home slowly, to start the horses' after-working cooling.

On this night, however, there was no respite; he continued to demand maximum speed though the horses' hampered breathing became an agonized loud honking. Outdoor servants heard them from a distance, along with the whip, still cracking like a rifle. All came running. When the coach stopped before the house, house servants rushed out to carry in the unharmed baby, the young wife, who had fainted, and the older woman who was in hysterics, incapable of sensible speech. Somebody went for the man who was father, husband and son.

One of the horses dropped in its tracks, convulsing, and its mate stood, blood gushing from its nose, struggling not to fall in the tangled harness amidst its companion's death throes. Charles turned at once to the team, but when he tried to undo them, made a terrible discovery; his fingers were limp, unworkable. As the archives put it, "his hands were all torn up...and the horses' mouths too. They could never be bitted again."

The story ended quietly, "There wasn't a mark on the horses but whip welts. The owner gave Charles a severe beating on the spot and told him to leave. A few days later, the driver's body surfaced in the lake. Other servants understood; his hands ruined, his job and reputation gone, the man's life was over. Before then, of course, the ladies had confirmed his story, but it was too late for Charles."

Nobody would have to guess the result. Sounds of the disastrous ride replay over and over for residents of that house and stories abound of ghostly encounters on the road through the canebrake. No sensible person would think of riding a horse on that road after dark.

Chapter Eighteen

The Illinois Slave House

He is not dead!
He only left
A precious robe of clay behind
To draw a robe of love and light
Around his disembodied mind.

Frances Ellen Watkins,
Nat. Anti-Slavery Standard, 1858

"We went knowing that it had been called 'a reverse underground railroad' because escapees were intercepted there and kidnapped freed people were held there. Still, I felt in such danger, just being in that place. I was almost sick with the need to be out of it."

The Missouri woman who told me this did not complete her tour of the 165-year-old Crenshaw House, located near Equality, Illinois. Ghost stories of the place, she said, center mainly on the wailing and moaning of imprisoned people and on the fact that although students from Southern Illinois University frequently undertake spending a night on the third floor as a dare, nobody has ever stuck it out.

Another Missourian overflowed with description and speculation. She said the top floor of the three-story house is devoted to stall-like rooms with barred openings, lining a narrow hallway.

"The guide told us they put as many as eight people in each of these," she said, "and it's beyond imagination. There would not be room for them to lie down or even sit. And how in the world do you suppose they managed the waste? They must have had periods when there were no prisoners and the family did its entertaining then, for we were told that Abraham Lincoln once was an overnight guest." My friend wondered, "How could he not have heard or smelled anything? There would surely have been sick and injured people who were too far out of it to be kept silent by threats."

And she empathized with all whose despair and physical sufferings must surely still saturate the place.

"Just imagine what it would be like to be an escaping slave, having already gone through no telling what kind of danger and exertion, probably hungry, being told they'd reached safety, a station on the road to freedom, and then be thrown into jail? Or to legally be free and have lived free in the north and then be captured and brought here to be sold back into slavery! But that wasn't the worst of it...." And she told us that the guide said John Hart Crenshaw was said to have systematically had every female captive impregnated before she was sent back south. Thus he could charge owners more for their return or sell them at a higher price.

For decades the truth of these rumors was not established. It was known that Crenshaw, a wealthy and respected farmer and businessman, had been sued at least twice for matters concerning slaves, but was not convicted either time. He owned many thousands of acres, "almost the whole southern tip of Illinois" my friend said. He used thousands of slaves, over time, in his salt mines and did so legally. Though illinois was officially a free state, its laws permitted leasing other peoples' slaves for such work as that in salt mines, an industry important to the state's economy. It would have been hard to prove that any slave in Crenshaw's hands was there illegally.

But now researchers seem to have evidence that some of the rumors were true. Of course there is no way to confirm every detail, but a November 26, 1999 edition of the *St. Louis Post Dispatch* reviewed the research, pictured the place and added these remarkable facts to its history:

Crenshaw's house was constructed so that a carriage could be driven inside and through it and could discharge passengers to staircases leading to the second floor — where the ballroom was — or on up to the third floor. This would have made possible the loading or unloading of slaves with minimum chance of anyone from the neighborhood being aware. The house formerly had a widow's walk, not common on inland houses, but this one enabled guards to watch for runaway slaves crossing the river. Then some of Crenshaw's slaves would be sent to welcome them and bring them to the house with promises of refuge.

In general, today, most psychics and psychic investigators put a rather reassuring spin on the supernatural. Though most admit that there can be dangerous negative aspects, they don't encourage our living in fear of evil spirits. However, Crenshaw's activity, if true, causing acute emotional and physical suffering for uncounted people for a period of many years surely would qualify as an example of pure evil. If anything justifies haunting, then the Crenshaw House is abundantly qualified to host many ghosts.

Chapter Nineteen

The Ultimate Apparition

Fog is the work of ghosts. Or ghosts are the work of fog.
Stephen Mooney

One of the all-time best accounts of an apparition came to me from a college days friend, Walter Darrell Haden, a Missourian now teaching in the University of Tennessee at Martin. This is not fiction. Darrell has described his experience to several large groups of colleagues. Several of his fellow workers have publicly discussed seeing what Darrell saw, with minor variations. We are not using their names here because not all of them can now be located to give permission.

The revenant was a man named Stephen Mooney, holder of a PhD, a college instructor in writing, the editor of a literary magazine named *The Tennessee Poetry Journal*, and poet-in-residence at University of Tennessee at Martin. He was the author of books of his own poetry and books about poetry.

Darrell met Mooney in June, 1967, at a teacher's conference at another Tennessee university, and in their conversation mentioned his desire to increase his teaching responsibilities and his income. Mooney told Darrell at once of a desirable opening where he himself taught. He invited Darrell to come and investigate. Their meeting had been an unusual one in several ways, the older man initiating it and making a few remarks that seemed to indicate supranormal knowledge about Darrell.

In about two weeks the former Missourian had been offered an appointment as assistant professor of English at UT Martin. He also had Mooney's invitation to share his home while the Hadens made a leisurely search for just the house they would want. The two men became close friends and after the Hadens settled near Fulton, Tennessee, Mooney was their frequent guest. He became much like a member of the family, helping with home improvements and calling himself "Uncle Steve" to their children. His status was walk-in-without-knocking, and nobody thought anything of Mooney's taking naps there or spending hours on the couch reading. He had similar — if not quite so close — relationships with several people at the university, all of whom sympathized with his loneliness and need for family.

Over the years, however, visiting gradually became less frequent. Darrell was completing graduate work at nearby Vanderbilt University and Mooney was busy with his publications and with setting up and securing prominent speakers for the Tennessee Poetry Circuit — which he founded — and such events as the state's Spring Poetry Festival. He used his own home to entertain the speakers, many of whom were nationally prominent.

While the friends were thus separated by work, Mooney suffered a heart attack and on May 12 of 1971, he died. His family in Alabama honored his request for cremation with ashes scattered in the gulf. Haden says that Mooney's passage left a void in the English department because so many people loved him as mentor and friend. Though work resumed as usual after a memorial service, the poet's presence had been such a strong and helpful one that teachers and students continued to talk to each other about him.

What happened to Darrell is more than worth this long introduction but could not be better told than in his own words. He is a highly qualified writer. Both popular and scholarly publications have used his work and he edits two scholarly magazines. Here's Darrell's story:

"Perhaps it was in late September of 1971, almost five months after his death, that I was lying on a throw rug in the family room at home, grading a set of student essays. Betty and the children had been in bed for an hour or more. As I recall, the time wasn't late, perhaps 10:20 in the evening. A cup of hot black coffee sat on a napkin on the hardwood floor within reach. It was not Irish coffee. I was fully alert, wide awake.

"Gradually, as I lay with my back to the couch, a strange feeling grew: I was not completely alone in the room. I glanced backward over my right shoulder. The sliding door was not cracked even a half-inch. Betty wasn't peeking through to ask how much longer I might be up and working, as she sometimes did when I worked past midnight.

"But there was something farther to the right of the closed door. I pivoted on my right elbow to look more closely. What I was about to see may have taken no more than ten to fifteen seconds.

"At the foot of the couch were what appeared to be brown oxford work shoes, these leaning against the lower arm of the couch.

"'Did I leave my shoes on the couch'? I wondered. 'When I slipped out of my shoes I must have kicked them off there'.

"Pivoting even farther on my right elbow and looking over my right shoulder, I saw now that there were brown socks in the shoes. These were not empty socks. When could the children have stuffed and placed

an effigy on the couch? I brought my right knee up and turned around in a kneeling position something less than six feet away from the couch. What I saw jerked me to my feet. I had never before, and I have never since had such an experience.

"Stretched full length in brown khaki trousers and shirt, Stephen Mooney lay on his back, his hands folded across his belt. He appeared to be sleeping. He did not look dead. There was as much color in his face as I remembered its having in life. His reading glasses were cocked high on his cranium. Light from the reading lamp reflected off his glossy bald head. The expression on his face looked only unconscious, neither pleasant nor unpleasant. In the few seconds I stood there, it was a benign apparition I saw.

"My heart was in my throat as I whirled and sprang toward the kitchen, narrowly missing — I noticed later — my coffee cup. Before I ran out the kitchen door and down four steep steps into the breezeway, I stopped, my hand on the door knob, to look back, still unsure of what I had witnessed.

"What I had just seen had faded from the feet up to the midriff. I could see orange couch through the lower half of the fast-fading apparition. But from the waist on up through his shining pate, the apparition still looked solid. I slammed the door and rushed out, gasping cool, fresh air. From the deep breezeway, I couldn't have looked — even if I had tried — through the high window into the corner of the room and the upper arm of the couch on which only a few seconds before I had seen Mooney's head resting.

"I was running down our driveway, sucking deeper breaths with each length I sprinted. I didn't look back. Apparently I wasn't thinking of my sleeping family. I thought only of putting more distance between me and what I had just seen. I ran completely around the new nine of the golf course just across from our farm.

"When I returned to the house half an hour later, I peered through the kitchen door that I opened only a crack. The couch looked as empty as it had when I lay down near it to grade papers. I examined the upper arm where the apparition's head had rested. How could I expect to find any indentation? Neither was there any other sign that what I had seen had ever been on the couch or anywhere else in the room. My cup and papers were still where I had left them. I emptied the cold coffee and woke Betty. She listened to the experience I have described here.

"'You've been working too hard,' she said. 'You've not been getting enough rest, Darrell.'

"The next morning when I wanted to talk more with her, my wife said, 'You may want to be careful who you tell this to. Not everyone will understand.'

"I did not tell anyone else until we attended a Halloween party a month or so later. Betty and I were guests along with other members of my department at the home of the university's new poet-in-residence, Victor Depta. Conversation turned gradually but ultimately to Victor's predecessor, this with no assist from me. Several of our colleagues speculated about Mooney's unusual gifts, his seeming psychic feats, his apparent clairvoyance and uncanny ability to read minds. But after all, hadn't he helped the U.S. Navy crack important Japanese codes? Then, too, had he not just published a new book of essays in Dublin — *The Grave of the Dwarf*?

"After I described the experiences I have given here, no one spoke for a few moments.

"Then the wife of one of my colleagues spoke her husband's name and asked, 'Do you remember late last spring when you had your Wednesday night class? It was raining hard. I went to the door when I heard someone open the screen door maybe fifteen minutes before I expected you home. I knew you had your key, so I didn't open. When I didn't hear your key in the lock I turned the outside light on and looked through the visor. A man in raincoat and rain hat was standing just a foot or two from me through the door. He was smoking a cigarette and just standing there. I could see by the light it looked like Mooney. I knew it couldn't be him, but I ran to the bathroom and locked myself in. The children were asleep. I didn't come out until I heard your key turn the tumbler a quarter hour later.'

"Next an adjunct faculty member from out of town spoke up, calling her husband by name. 'Honey, I've been planning to tell you this, but I couldn't — not until now. I saw Mooney at our door one afternoon late this summer. I was watching through the curtain of a window in the next room. He knocked two or three times before he turned around and walked back to the street. If you had been there with me, I might have thought about opening the door.'

"We were to learn of nine or ten other sightings of Mooney reportedly occurring immediately before and shortly after those described at the party. One of Mooney's proteges and a graduate student in Memphis reported encountering the apparition in that city. Another, in graduate school in Nashville, said he saw Mooney there. Two of Steve's former students told me in Paris, Tennessee that each had seen, independent of the other, what appeared to be Mooney in that city. A year or two later, a married couple who had met first in the poet's class reported a joint viewing of his apparition in their home in Lake County. Both alumni still teach in the public schools near Reelfoot Lake.

"When Robert Bly returned to our campus twenty years after Mooney had first brought him there to read, my chairman asked me to introduce Steve's long-time friend to a large audience. However, before I could begin, the poet asked me to tell about my experience with the apparition of Mooney. 'I'd like to hear it again,' he said.

"After I told the audience what I have recalled here, I introduced our speaker. Bly turned to me and said for all his audience to hear 'Walt, you should be comforted you saw Mooney at peace. Apparently he loved your family and your home. Perhaps Mooney wanted to let you know he is all right. Be proud you had this experience. Not everyone has such an opportunity.'

"Some eight years later, when I went back to Mooney's *Grave of the Dwarf* and *News From the South*, I found passages I could not remember reading before. Both books are much animated by apparitions, but it is 'The Guide's Speech', from the former work that has given me the greatest pause:

'To be a successful apparition...
Be tangible in a few expert ways.
And most of all, believe: Always believe
That you are real.
Have a real face,
With eyes. And hands, each hand uniquely
Veined; the patterns must not match.
Some evidence of struggle, a personal mark,
A scar on the thumb or at the edge
Of the cheek-bone will be persuasive,
                        Stimulating
Images of falls in childhood and normal
Adolescent accidents with knives.
...inner organs do not matter in our usual
Public appearances; they will be assumed.
Expand your clothing to its proper curve
And line. Bend, bow and kneel. Everyone
Will think you a sensible creature,

Pouched with life, rounded and bounded
And bagged and bundled with life.
      So designed,
You may descend to find what you shall find.'"

> *I can call up old ghosts, and they*
> *will come. But my art limps;*
> *I cannot send them home.*
> Stevie Smith, *Old Ghosts*

> *Out of oblivion*
> *Into the fear of oblivion*
> *Back to oblivion.*
> Paul Grimes, *The Circle of Life*

In Addition

Some ghostly material is hard to sort. Does what we know is fiction belong with what is presented as true and may really be true? What about individuals who can answer some of our questions about the unknown? They're not ghosts and they're not telling us ghost stories, but ghost buffs usually are very interested in what these people say. And what about the folklore and customs with which our forebears — for centuries back — tried to handle what no mortal understands? Many readers of *Missouri Ghost* have offered material of this sort, often saying in effect, "it's all related, isn't it?"

So here's some of the unsortable. If it doesn't seem to you to belong here, just read the epilogue and close the book. But you may be missing something!

Chapter Twenty

Short Takes

*Ghosts! There are nigh a thousand million walking the
earth openly at noontide. O Heaven, it is mysterious, it
is awful to consider that we not only carry each a future
ghost within, but are, in very deed, ghosts!*
                                            Thomas Carlyle

A great many short takes on the supernatural are
offered by people attending book-promoting events.
Some of the most intriguing of these short stories have
almost no details. Many, despite their brevity, give new
perspective on the unexplainable. The following samples
fit a variety of categories.

Lisa "Charlie" Thomas of Columbia, who knew the
late Ashland ghost-seeker Russ Hawkins very well, says
he maintained that despite all the supposedly haunted
houses he'd investigated, he'd never seen a ghost. His
stories were memorable, however, especially one about
time gone berserk. He said that in the 1880s an Ashland
man set out to walk to Columbia, a routine event in those
days. He never returned home, however, and never was
heard from again. Fifty years later, a man turned up in
Columbia who claimed to be this person. He could not
explain where he had been and he had the appearance of
a man in his thirties.

A woman reared in Ashland said that as children, she and her brother, sharing a bedroom, were often awakened by the sound of somebody chopping wood. She said they didn't dream this, but lay awake listening and whispering about it. She also said that once a strange figure appeared in their room, but vanished quickly when her brother crossly told it to go away. This woman commented that two or three houses burned on the site of her childhood home and that her aunt later lived in one built there, but never mentioned anything unusual happening.

Men who participate in Civil War reenactments often describe eerie feelings of being in or near another time. They attribute this to their standing on the site where a battle took place — perhaps an engagement their forebears knew. Many reenactors make a special effort to go where their ancestors were — wearing the same clothes worn then, their stomachs containing the same kind of food, in their hands weapons that may have seen action in that very place. Some describe a near-panic, feeling that they could step into the past if they wanted to or might inadvertently fall into it.

One reenactor told me of reading about slits in the fabric of time; the writer he quoted said that we could pass through a slit if we turned sideways at exactly the right place, and moved in the right direction. Something like that must have happened at Inspiration Point near Branson. Since 1962 a barely visible horseman reportedly has been seen fleeing from reenactors or film actors in scenes depicting Baldknobbers in pursuit. Inspiration Point was a lookout post during the War.

One of the original dirty old men is said to haunt bathrooms at Lake House in Hollister. Described as ashen-faced, with stringy grey hair and a lecherous expression, he peers into windows 18 feet off the ground. Local legend is that he's the ghost of a man who had sins more serious than window-peeping; he supposedly murdered his wife and children in the basement of the house.

A barefooted woman carrying a baby and limping over ridges of the Ozarks Mountains is thought to be the spirit of a woman named Laurie May, who in 1930 was the victim of spousal abuse. In a struggle with her husband their baby was dropped and died of concussion. The man then killed Laurie May.

An extended Cole County family included a spinster great-aunt who refused to live in the house with the others, or even to eat with them except on the most festive occasions. For special meals she would leave her chosen quarters in a former summer kitchen and accept a plate on the porch, where one or two of the others would keep her company. The reason for this eccentricity?   "I don't want to be around that clock," she said. The clock she disliked was a large ornate "grandfather" type much cherished by several generations of the family. Supposedly it had once, as the song says, stopped short, at the very moment of a patriarch's death. The family had accepted that as coincidence, especially since, over the years, it never happened again. Yet when the great-aunt died in a Jefferson City hospital, the carefully tended, regularly wound clock in the family home stopped at exactly the hour given on her death certificate.

Elsewhere in this book we quote an undated but obviously old issue of a St. Joseph newspaper. Here's one more short story from that source.
   A stooped, gray-clad woman used to be seen in the city cemetery in early morning hours, before full light had come. She seemed to be going from grave to grave,

reading tombstones. The explanation given is that this is the spirit of a woman who killed a young man and soon after died unexpectedly. She went to her own grave unrepentant, a classic circumstance of many ghost stories. Some say, according to the newspaper, that because she had no opportunity to learn remorse or to pay for her sin, her spirit is doomed to search perpetually for the victim's grave. When she finds it, she can seek forgiveness.

At a St. Louis book signing, a woman told me how she gets rid of a rocking chair ghost in the empty apartment above her. She puts on heavy boots and stomps around, which always outrages the man in the apartment beneath her. He has a remarkably strong voice and a richly profane vocabulary. His shouting at her quiets the ghost upstairs.

Another St. Louisan told of a house just off Arsenal street, a house with a staircase that ended in a blank wall. Nothing unusual happened there when the husband was home, just with the family, and nothing very dramatic when he was away and the others were there alone. However, if male visitors came into the house, whether or not the husband was there, heavy winds swept through, banging doors angrily and footsteps pounded up and down the basement stairs. When residents looked, of course there was nothing to see. The house also had the problem of basement lights coming back on after being turned off.

Still another St. Louis woman told me of a kitchen ordeal she'd had since her husband died. He had been very resentful of the limited diet he had to live with and which she had conscientiously forced on him. Now, whenever she fixes some of the foods he most liked, forbidden to him in his last illness, pans and dishes rattle on their shelves. His illness had also forced him to stop smoking in the last years of his life, yet she often smells cigarette smoke.

Joyce O'Neal's October, 1997 column in *Ozark Senior Living* published in Springfield, tells of a baffling incident in her Ozarks family. "We heard a terrific crash. It sounded like the roof fell onto the upstairs floor and we expected to see sky through the upstairs ceiling, but nothing was even out of place."

A sample of how different, unforgettable and eerie Robbie Courtaway got in *Spirits of St. Louis:* One of her sources, Frank Schumgai, was the son of a stonemason who had been employed to evaluate the foundation of a large old building slated for renovation. He, with the owners, found an almost indescribable complex of space under the house, including a sub-cellar with floor forty feet beneath the ground, this entered through a well-like portion from which doors led into several corridors and rooms. Lower levels had apparently connected with the network of caves used by St. Louis brewers for storage, but were blocked off by remarkably stout doors and brick barriers.

Climax to this evaluation tour was the appearance of something that did not seem real, yet was not an apparition, something obviously alive and intent on escaping from the cellars. We'll leave further details on that for readers to discover for themselves from Courtaway's book.

Chapter Twenty One

Pure Fabrications

*ghost stories...while I doubt any one of them, still
I have faith in the whole of them taken together.*
Immanuel Kant, *Dream of a Spirit Seer*

People who relay ghost stories are often accused of
— at best — adding frills and embroidery. At worst,
we're accused of outright lies and we probably do inadvertently pass along some untruths. Anyone who collects
ghost stories realizes that many storytellers can't resist
adding a clever or poignant touch. We have to fight it
ourselves, even though we try to stay with the essence
which may shed new light on the unknown.

Here are two short stories by Missourians. The first,
published in Autumn, 1994, in *Country Folk Magazine* is
fictionalized speculation about just what might have
occurred in author Ronnie Powell's home area to bring
about a tragedy which underlies many reports of eerie
encounters near Windyville, the haunted town he
described in an earlier chapter. The second story
appeared in 1999 in *Columbia Senior Times*.
Occasionally such experiences as Holder writes of are
related as true and as seeming evidence of time slip.

The Ghost Of Dugan Lane

by Ronnie Powell

*That house is not fit to live in. No one's been able
to live in it. It doesn't want people.*
Mina Handry, The Changeling

A narrow dirt road leads away to the south from
Highway M, a mile west of Windyville, Missouri. This
road is known as Dugan Lane. After leaving the highway,
the lane disappears into a shroud of trees as it follows the
east bank of Indian Creek. Not far down the lane, at the
base of a hill, once stood a large two-story log dwelling.
A wide front porch graced the front of the old structure
and a huge stone fireplace rested against the east end. In
front of the house stood a small open-fronted building,
within whose gloomy realm was a low, stone-walled,
hand-dug well. Across the road, east of the house, stood
a large barn, constructed of native stone and oak lumber.
This property was once the homestead of John Dugan.

Several years after the Dugan family moved away,
another family took up residence, a young couple, Emil
and Amanda, and their infant daughter, Roberta. Amanda
was a strikingly handsome woman, tall, fair of skin and
wore her dark, shoulder length hair unbound. It is said
that she possessed a smile as warm as sunshine and eyes
as bright and innocent as a blue spring sky. She was
content, they say, delighted to be a wife and mother. She
enjoyed tending to household chores and working in the
garden.

On a certain fateful day in April, she awakened early,
as usual, and slipped quietly from the bed she shared
with Emil. Careful not to disturb her husband, Amanda
tiptoed across the floor to where Roberta lay sleeping in

her crib. Gently she picked up the little girl and crept softly down the stairs to the kitchcn. She sat the child down on the floor, then began preparing the morning meal. Soon the fragrances of biscuits baking and bacon frying filled the room. Roberta, meantime, enjoyed her freedom. Her attention was drawn to a cricket hopping about near the outer doorway of the kitchen. Intent on catching the insect she began crawling, rising to her feet at times. Coming ever closer to the elusive creature, she was steadily drawing nearer to the open door.

Preoccupied with her duties, Amanda did not notice her daughter's pursuit. Humming softly to herself, she placed on the table a steaming platter of bacon and eggs, a bowl of oatmeal and finally, a covered pan of biscuits.

Still unnoticed by her mother, Roberta toddled out the door onto the front porch. Slowly, with uncertain strides, the child made her way to the steps, sat and scooted down each stone, until she reached the ground. Once again she stood on wobbly legs and then began the short journey to the well house. A few moments later she dropped to her knees and crawled inside the damp enclosure.

Roberta pulled herself up with little difficulty and with childish curiosity peered into the dark expanse of the well. The shimmering water far below caught her reflection and, perhaps reaching toward it, she leaned farther out over the edge of the stone wall. Suddenly she lost her hold and toppled headlong.

The baby's cries reverberated loudly up from the dark deep hole, then ended abruptly. Nevertheless, they had reached Amanda. She momentarily stood paralyzed with fear, then ran from the kitchen, nearly tripping on the hem of her night gown. Frantically she called Roberta, but no answer came. She ran toward the well house, just as Emil appeared on the porch. Amanda's voice reached a terrible pitch as she frantically scanned the yard around her.

Blindly she stumbled inside the well house and threw herself to the edge of the dark shaft, only to glimpse a tiny hand slipping beneath the water. Screaming hysterically, completely overwhelmed, Amanda sank backward and fainted.

They came, many friends and relatives for several days and probed the well for Roberta's body, but their efforts were futile and one by one they gave up. All the while, Amanda sat on the porch, weeping and pleading for the return of her beloved daughter. She refused to accept Roberta's death. She refused to give up her hopeless vigil for several days and remained on the porch, still clothed in the now soiled white night gown. But as days passed, she appeared to accept the tragic loss and life went on.

In the latter part of June, several weeks following Roberta's drowning, Amanda rose from her bed to a morning fragrant with lilac bloom. Careful not to waken Emil, she descended to the kitchen and began preparing the morning meal as usual, humming all the while. When the food was ready, she called out softly for Emil to come.

He was pleased that Amanda had at last come to terms with her grief, but ate hurriedly, for there was much work to do. Afterward, Amanda followed him to the roadside, gently kissed him and watched him harness his team and head for a nearby corn field.

Amanda turned then, slowly as if preoccupied, and began walking across the lawn. She stopped short of the porch steps and stood for a time watching Emil cultivating corn. A playful breeze tugged mischievously at the white grown she wore and teased her flowing hair. Tears welled up in Amanda's eyes and ran freely down her

cheeks. She began walking toward the well house, slowly at first, but quickening her pace and without hesitation stepped inside the building. The sun, having topped the crest of a ridge, gently pushed aside the darkness within. Its light revealed Amanda leaning out over the low wall, weeping brokenly, sobbing loudly, staring into the inky water below. Suddenly she sprang. Her gown belled out and her hair streamed upward, hiding her tear stained face. Cold water quickly pulled her down into its dark depths. They found Amanda's body with little difficulty and a day later buried it in a church cemetery not far from where she perished. Emil, devastated by a second untimely loss, left the farm, and in time his tragedies seemed forgotten in the neighborhood. The house remained empty, however, for no one relished the thought of living there. Amanda's garden soon succumbed to weeds and the house became a lonely sight.

One summer night a year or so after Amanda's and Roberta's deaths, a man riding a horse along the tree-roofed lane was confronted by the sudden appearance of a tall, fair skinned woman, clothed in a white gown. Long unbound hair glistened in the moonlight, but her face was distorted as if in agony. She stood near the center of the road, arms outstretched beseechingly, weeping unashamedly. The horse, terrified, bolted, throwing its rider. He scrambled to his feet and though gasping for breath and suffering minor injures, fled the scene. That man, of unquestionable character and honesty, never wavered in his account of what he saw one dreadful night. Until his death years later, he swore that the ghostly image he saw was that of Amanda. And, it's said that the horse who shared his experience could never again be ridden.

Amanda was sighted again several months later, early one morning standing on the porch of the house, clothed in the gown, an unearthly glow around her face and hair. It was said that she entered the house and could be seen with a lighted lamp, climbing stairs to the loft.

The last known sighting of Amanda occurred nearly fifteen years after her death. A young woman walking along the road observed a woman, pale of face with long dark hair, clothed in a white gown to her feet, standing just outside the well house. She stood with arms outstretched, weeping.

The old barn finally gave way to neglect and fell in a splintered heap of wood and twisted tin. Sometime later, during the darkness of night, the house and the building that covered the well mysteriously got on fire. The remaining rubble was bulldozed over the well.

All that remains of Amanda's world at present is a weed grown meadow and a tree shrouded lane. But I wonder: is she still searching at the edge of eternity for Roberta?

The Dedham Moors Inn

by Harold Holder

Time is but the river I am fishing in...
Its current slides away, but eternity remains.
David Henry Thoreau

The great Polish writer, Joseph Conrad, once said, "Never fear the supernatural; rather fear man, for he is capable of every evil there is." I am not superstitious nor do I believe in ghosts, yet there is no explanation for the perplexing tale I am about to relate. Critics tell us that the worst opening for a story is "It was a dark and stormy night...." Be that as it may, how else shall I begin this tale?

It was a dark and stormy night as I sat gazing through the dirty, rain-drenched panes of a single small window in the gray and brooding.... But now, tonight, as I sit at home in my comfortable study, I can recall it as if it were yesterday. Let me take you back when my story began, three months ago:

It happened as I was on a cycling tour in a sparsely populated area of northern England. I was photographing ancient castles and ruins in a desolate region and found myself on lonely Dedham Moors Road. Night was descending and a rain storm was approaching, thus I was forced to seek shelter in an old inn which with great difficulty I could see in the encroaching fog. A feeling of dread overcame me as I neared the door of the inn, its gray stone walls hoary with age. After I had pounded on the door several times, it opened a crack and a raspy voice said, "Can't tha see w'shut?"

I could hardly understand his dialect, but pleaded with him to let me take shelter from the rain which began to fall at that moment. He said, "Sod off," but a female voice from behind him seemed to be arguing on my side. After considerable exchange in their puzzling dialect, he opened the door to me, but said with a scowl that they would not feed me and I'd have to pay twenty guineas in advance. That's nearly fifty dollars in American money, but it was worth it, to get shelter.

The woman led the way upstairs and I thanked her as I was shown into quarters consisting of two small rooms with no bath and no light but one oil lamp. The first room had a single small window and was appointed simply, with an old brass bed, one chair and a small table. A porcelain chamber pot under the bed completed the furnishings. As for the other room, it was entirely devoid of furniture and its windowless walls held no pictures or mirrors. Both rooms were uncarpeted, but they were unaccountably warm. I saw no fireplace or signs of a central heating system. Halfheartedly, I was checking my photo equipment when I heard a strange noise. Seeing nothing out of the ordinary in the lonely room, I thought it must have been the raging storm outside. Shortly after returning to the task at hand, I experienced a chill, but not a blast of cold air. It was more like when you open a freezer door and the cold creeps and flows slowly around you. I had a dire feeling that something was not right, but knowing that the door and window were secured fast, I could not fathom this sensation. Turning once again to the door of the other room, I thought I saw a movement in the darkness beyond. Taking up the oil lamp, I looked into the room, but saw nothing there. Placing the lamp on the table, I noticed what strange shadows its flame cast on the wall. These, and the open doorway, with nothing beyond, suggested to me an intriguing photograph. Adjusting my camera, I took a shot. Nothing untoward occurred during the rest of the night.

After a fitful sleep, I arose early, gathered my equipment and went downstairs. No one was about and after calling out several times, I left the inn. Sometime during the night, the storm had ended and now sunlight was bright. Retrieving my cycle, I noticed that the ground was not wet. Surely, after such a downpour, there should be pools of water, but the heath was not even damp. Eager to be on my way, I shrugged off the anomaly and pedaled away. A few yards down the road, I stopped and took three shots of the old inn. They would make an interesting addition to my collection.

Back home, I developed the rolls of film, all of which came out beautifully, except for the one that held the Dedham Moors Inn pictures. The photo of the door to the empty room was there, but those of the inn's exterior startled me. They contained part of the road and the moors beyond, but the Dedham Moors Inn was not there. I remembered that the sun had been bright that morning, and my exposure settings correct. The inn was not there.

I wrote to a British friend and asked him if he would go to Dedham Moors Road, find the inn, take a snapshot and send it to me. He wrote back that he had traveled that road, ten kilometers from one end to the other, but there was not a building on the entire length, not even a shed. How can that be? It wasn't a dream. I had the photo of the doorway.

Upon examining it further, in the darkened doorway I saw two red dots that should not have been there. There had been nothing to cause a reflection in the lens, no flaw in the negative and no double exposure. What could they be? I took a magnifying glass and examined them. What I saw made my hair stand on end and sent a cold chill over me. It was unmistakable.... Six inches below the top of the doorway, staring back at me, were two red eyes!

Holder's note: Although this fiction is set in England, the photo that inspired it — a photo showing two red eyes — was actually taken in an abandoned farm house in Osage County, Missouri. The lady who took the picture and looked at the two red dots with a magnifying glass was so frightened by what she saw that she immediately destroyed the photo and negative.

Chapter Twenty Two

Ask Bevy Jaegers

The so-called supernatural is perfectly natural.
Bevy Jaegers

The statement above is only one of several that Bevy Jaegers of St. Louis says she has coined to try to clarify public thinking about some of the things we don't fully understand. Another is "extended sensory perception" rather than extra sensory perception, for Jaegers is deeply convinced that we all have the capacity to extend our senses without the need for elaborate otherworldly processes.

Jaegers feels she is proof of this for she was not born with remarkable perceptions, as some people claim to be. She developed hers through study and experimentation, thus believes that anyone else who chooses to can do the same. In the interest of clarity, Jaegers rejects the term "psychic" for herself, substituting the more concrete "psychic investigator". She sometimes adds that she has learned to be a competent remote viewer, just as most of us could do. Remote viewing takes perception beyond what is immediate and apparent and can result in accurate predictions.

"The reason I don't want to be called a psychic," she says, "is because that's a word with a lot of baggage. People expect tricks and drama, a theatrical looking

person who probably is basically an entertainer. As an investigator, I'm trying to find the cause and meaning of unusual happenings, and to report these in a scientific manner that cannot be dismissed as mumbo-jumbo."

Jaegers also rejects the word "occult" because its common interpretation is as a synonym for evil activity. Actually in most dictionaries, occult's first definition is "hidden." Similarly, Jaegers has come to dislike supernatural, supranormal, paranormal and other words implying that human mental and emotional capacities — except in a few elite individuals — are static and severely limited. She has devoted her adult life to helping people learn how to make full use of the senses they were born with. She works by writing for publication and by conducting workshops and seminars and lecturing throughout the U. S. For the last few decades, she's been among the most-written-of psychic investigators in the United States. She's written of in other countries, too, and people from abroad have attended her seminars.

But what does all this have to do with ghosts? In her early days of self education, Bevy participated in group activity focused on investigation of the unusual, and helping people who felt they were in the grip of troublesome spirits. She still helps in such situations from time to time, but mainly now in an advisory role. Yet here again, she sees a need to change the language. "I prefer the term 'entity,'" she says and then explains that there are many differing types of beings and manifestations.

What we bundle up as ghosts are to her spirits of several types. Some are what she terms the intelligent remains of people who, from circumstances of a sudden death, don't realize they are dead and are continuing the usual routines of their lives. Some are spirits reluctant to go on to another stage of existence because they fear Hell or have some mission to complete here or guilt to work off. "Such cases are rare," she comments.

Danger from ghosts? Jaegers says that apart from fiction and legend, she's never heard of a ghost hurting anyone. Bevy has known of people hurting themselves in panicked flight. She says that most entities are unaware of and uninterested in us. She agrees with those who say that time glitches of several types account for some of what seems ghostly to us.

Methods of self-protection: "If you feel that an unseen presence is with you," Jaegers says, "pray for control of your own fear and for the peace of the spirit." She has been quoted many times with the formula she and her investigating team have used: "We say to the entity, 'Put out your hand and look for the light. It will take you to a better place.' I don't know exactly why this works, but in most cases it seems to."

Bevy Jaegers does not believe in possession. She has often said that what we must worry about is *OB*session that comes of dabbling in the unknown during a bereavement or in other stressful times. She advocates being careful what we let into our lives, which means having nothing to do with seances, ouija boards, and automatic writing. (Unlike many advisors, however, Jaegers accepts tarot cards as "only a focus for concentration, not dangerous.") She says that a great many predatory "spiritualist" charlatans take advantage of people's need for comfort and that we should never get involved with those who offer readings or mediumistic sessions for pay, then warn of dangerous conditions that they can fend off for us if we pay them special fees.

Jaegers' approach to what she doesn't want to call the supernatural has always been critical and pragmatic. "I've been interested," she says, "in finding what can be proved and documented." And she has never been as interested in exorcising ghosts as she was in learning how our natural powers can be extended to enhance our lives. "Only a Roman Catholic priest can do exorcisms," she states.

To people who feel compelled, during a bereavement, to try to make contact with a loved one, Jaegers says that perhaps during the period before the funeral, our love and prayers — offered without need for an intermediary — can be felt by those we are reluctant to lose. After that, she feels we should free the spirits so they can turn without impediment to what they need to do in the hereafter.

Bevy advises against individuals going out alone and uninformed looking for ghosts. Her own work has usually been with a group of trained investigators whose methods are objective and professional. They are known as the St, Louis Psi Squad. "Our group originally started," Bevy says, "to rescue people who had got themselves into an unwholesome state with experimenting and had already exhausted the help of ministers and others. Some actually did have unpleasantness going on. Poltergeists, usually."

Poltergeists, Bevy Jaegers says, are not ghosts or spirits or anything except discharged kinetic energy. She says the activity usually stems from "unexpressed anger or frustration from young people, perhaps hormonal in nature, and usually ends in a few weeks, whether or not the family attempts to take action."

Instead of calling in psychics and priests, she believes parents should look to the emotional needs of their children, if poltergeists seem to be present. Helping children with whatever troubles them, whatever makes them want extra attention, may end the disturbances. Sometimes children have been caught in the act of engineering the weird effects laid to poltergeists. Whatever is going on needs to be looked at critically from the beginning, Bevy says, with an eye for how it could be staged. Most families are too alarmed when strange things happen to take a skeptical and analytical attitude.

A great deal of Jaegers' work involves her with the scientific community, for she has been for several years more journalist than anything else. She sells regularly to national magazines devoted to her interests — archeology and antiques among others — and in the last few years she has sold books on her hobby, hands, to Berkley in New York. The titles *Beyond Palmistry, I* and *II*, give a hint on content. She has done another book on fingerprints and how they reveal character, a theory now accepted and utilized by some law enforcers. Her latest book, *The Write Stuff* from Krause, is about antique pens and ink wells.

Among books Bevy self-published in the past for people attending her workshops is *Psychometry, Science of Touch*, particularly useful to anyone studying extension of senses. The work that gives Bevy most satisfaction is classes held for law enforcement and military teams who need to extend their sensory capability. For decades she has regularly assisted police by using her own extended and heightened senses to help locate missing persons, dead bodies, and perpetrators of crimes. She comes from what police call "a police family," her father, grandfather, uncle and brother all having been on the force. She herself is a licensed private detective, which enables her to testify as expert witness in cases she's involved with; a private citizen "psychic" could not.

Here's one of Bevy Jaegers' most publicized police cases: In 1971, a St Louis woman named Sally Lucas had been missing for eight weeks. When Bevy agreed to work with the case, she was given a nightgown and powder puff of Mrs. Lucas' to see what impressions she might get from them. An intimation of death surprised Bevy when she first placed the gown across her arm. Feeling that anything coming so quickly was probably not valid, she put the garment aside for several hours and then tried again. Once more she had the certainty of death and with a few added details, images of the letter C and of horses. She was sure that the woman had been dead before she was reported missing and that her body still was in the Metropolitan St. Louis area.

Then one of Jaegers' pupils, Jim Mueller, called to tell her he'd had what he called "a vision" of driving in a car on a winding country road and ending up somewhere near a stream close to the Missouri River. He felt the site was Babler State Park, a place off Highway 40 that he knew well. Together they went there and hiked around for about half an hour. The young man had no further impressions, but Bevy felt sure Mrs. Lucas' body was near. The area was densely grown up, including, she said, weeds that were shoulder high. She and her pupil went twice to the area and spent hours there. Jaegers still felt they were near Mrs. Lucas' body.

Meanwhile, the woman's car had been discovered in Florida and brought back to St. Louis. When given an opportunity to sit in it, Bevy felt sure, while in the driver's seat that the victim had been hit on the right side of her face and strangulation attempted but not completed. Sitting on the passenger side, she was certain that the attacker had been a dark-haired man.

Mrs. Lucas was found within ten feet of where Jaegers had repeatedly walked. Police were amazed that Bevy had been almost 100% accurate about the injuries and about the location of the victim, on Highway C and Wild Horse Creek Road. Reading such experiences inspires curiosity about the everyday life of such a person as Bevy Jaegers, but she insists that in most ways she's quite average. She's mother, grandmother and great grandmother, a collector of books and certain antiques, and a writer. Bevy Jaegers insists that she is not a psychic.

Chapter Twenty Three

Missouri Omens

"A wild bird in the house means someone will die. That's what Ma always said." My own mother whispered this as she stood carefully on a chair, dish towel in hand, eyes intent on a chimney sweep who had blundered into the room and clung against new wallpaper. This happened often enough that my mother grew adept at flinging a towel over a bird with one hand while the other grasped it through the cloth, too gently to hurt it, but firmly enough to get it out the door.

"The person who'll die," my dad commented, "might be the one who teeters and stretches around after the bird. Better a few soot stains than a broken back."

Probably this is how folklore has always been passed along, half-belief tempered by hardy realism. But nothing could keep people from repeating their elders' pronouncements, which most frequently regarded death, that great unsolved mystery, and were looked upon as messages from the other side.

"There'll be two more, if you'll notice," a family friend named Aunt Sis used to say confidently about any unusual death — a suicide, a new mother, an accident to a child or young person. "Just watch," she'd say.

And it proved true in our town occasionally. One summer three children died in various ways and a year or two later came a trilogy of suicides. But psychologists now declare that one suicide often triggers others in depressed individuals. Maybe other deaths subtly diminish the assumption of continued life in certain people. Surely the death of one teenager proves to others that they are not really immortal. The death of a new mother reminds all who are pregnant that they're irreversibly committed to something possibly fatal. Who can guess the effects in days when life was far more fragile than today? Instead of condescendingly talking about superstition, perhaps we should say, "How brave our forebears were, facing the unknown armed with little but their observations and speculations!"

Vance Randolph, in his book *Ozark Magic and Folklore*, devotes a chapter to how anxiously our ancestors watched for warnings of death and tried to avert the grim reaper. A sampling:

A picture or a window sash falling of its own accord could mean death hovered over the home. The same warning lay in unusual sounds from clock workings, or something inexplicable, such as a stopped clock that suddenly began to chime, or an object that broke when nobody was near it. Some claimed to have been warned of death by a sound of breaking glass where no glass was, or the sound of cloth being ripped.

Breaking a needle while quilting could mean the quilter would die before the quilt was done or before it wore out (not such a dire prediction, actually, considering the life expectancy of a quilt). A bath just before traveling was foolish; it could invite death by drowning, somewhere far from home.

🐾 Illness in the household meant that special care must be taken in several ways. This was not the time to make new clothes for the afflicted person, or to sweep the floor under their bed. Chances of recovery might be estimated by touching a piece of bread to the patient's lips and then throwing it to the dog. If the dog declined it, death was certain. One wonders how many indifferently fed dogs of pioneer times ever refused a piece of bread!

🐾 The doings of animals provided many of Randolph's listed death omens. If either wild or domestic creatures behaved out of character — say a whippoorwill calling from a rooftop or a rooster crowing on the doorstep — residents might be very frightened. A dog who rolled over and over in the same direction was said to be "measuring his master's grave."

Randolph's collection, of course, missed many omens. To Native tribes the sight of a shooting star meant that a soul was leaving earth. Pioneers adopted this belief, even specifying whether the soul was bound for Heaven or Hell, depending on whether the angle of the star's descent was left or right. Old timers insisted that war always brought unusual numbers of shooting stars; they'd seen it happen.

One elder's shared experience demonstrates why people clung to these beliefs: they saw, or thought they saw, confirmation. She told of disbelieving in death-watch beetles, until the night she spent at the bedside of an aged man whose death was eminent. On the night that proved to be his last, those sitting with him heard strong, distinctive clicking sounds from the walls, moving about all four sides of the room, overhead, and from the floor too. Those present looked at each other and nodded knowingly, or whispered "the death watch."

My relative told me these sounds stopped just as someone touched the man's throat and mouthed, "He's gone." The sounds did not resume. She said, "There was no dry wall or other interior covering of any kind on the logs of this house, no surface for insects' feet to click over, and nothing to conceal them if they were running around. And the way the sound moved, never coming from two spots at the same time...it moved around too fast to have been any insect we knew of."

Dreams

Dreams were particularly strong omens to pioneers, and even in the present, we're often unsettled by those that seem to foretell something unpleasant. In childhood I believe I heard more people comparing dreams than I hear today, though.

Pauline Ernst of Dixon, whose people lived their lives in the Ozarks says that her grandmother told her several times of dreams that seemed to foretell death.

"I'd be with someone in a dream," the older woman said, "and they would turn their back to me, not answering when I spoke. Sometimes they would turn away and look out a window, or just open a door and leave. If we were outdoors, they might walk off or start doing some little task as if I weren't there. Sometimes I'd know they couldn't talk because they were crying."

Pauline's father told a poignant prophetic dream. He said that when he was young he left the farm to work in

St. Louis and soon felt he was becoming a real city man, seldom thinking of homefolk and the life he'd left behind. Then one night, he dreamed this:

"I was standing at my usual bus stop and everything seemed real as could be. Suddenly my old dog from home came running up, our working farm dog who helped to raise me. He'd been old when I left home and not much to me for some time before that. But there he was in St. Louis, looking fit and pretty, like when he was young, and he was so happy to see me. He jumped up and turned in circles and did all he used to do. He barked and his voice was the same as always, so very clear, bringing back the farm and all, sounding sweet to me. I knelt down and hugged him and could really feel his body. I woke up crying because I'd paid so little attention to him in my last years at home and here he'd taken the trouble to follow me to the city!"

Those feelings grew into remorse for being so thoughtless about the home he had left and next day he wrote to his mother. Before the week was out came a reply telling him, among other news, that Shep had died; it had happened, as we might expect, the very night of the dream.

Feather Crowns

The pioneer clue about death that fascinated Vance Randolph most was the "feather crowns" or "angel wreaths" found in pillows and taken as a promise that a golden crown awaited the pillow's user.

Randolph quotes several people in detail about the wreaths they found and describes the twenty or so he saw. These ranged from firm circlets to what might almost have been the remains of a sloppy bird nest. What impressed him most was large, solid, bun-like masses of feathers, concave on top and bottom, sides as neat as those on a manufactured pill box hat. He cold see no evidence that any of these were man-made. In some, the feathers were strongly and neatly connected, almost as if interwoven. Some contained human hair and fibers from bedding. All crowns were highly cherished by owners. He saw one displayed in a glass-topped walnut box constructed for the purpose.

Katherine Henry of Rockaway Beach has a special interest in feather crowns because she found one in the pillow of her late husband. Mrs. Henry shows this crown to school children as a part of programs she does to pass along some historical sidelights that texts usually miss. She sent me an article by Bessie Foster of Galena, whose family found two thin crowns in the pillow of a young boy who died suddenly in 1914 of appendicitis. Mrs. Foster said one of these was about two inches across, the other twice as wide. Both were about an inch thick. She proclaimed both of them beautiful and reminded her readers that crowns might be forming in their pillows at that moment.

Many writers have tried to explain these wreaths, the most common speculation being that continual pressure from a sleeper's head and the adhering qualities of feathers would be likely to create something, depending on moisture and heat present and on how much the pillow was turned and shaken or otherwise disturbed. Naturally a person sick in bed for a long time, perhaps feverish and perspiring a lot, would have greatest potential for creating a crown.

Housewives usually scalded feathers before using them in pillows and perhaps it was hard to get these completely dry; with moisture in them, they might be quite prone to clump up. My mother never said she was trying to prevent formation of feather crowns, but her treatment of pillows — daily vigorous pummeling — suggests it, as does her ritual of annually opening and washing ticks.

Feathers were released into a clean wash tub and sunned all day, thoroughly stirred several times. This was a messy, tedious chore, especially when it was time to repack ticks. She greeted nylon and then kapok pillows with delight, having always considered feather pillows unclean. As with so many of our elders' feelings, my mother's now are confirmed by health authorities, allergists especially. Angel crowns or wreaths probably could not form in today's expensive pillows and would get no attention if they did.

Safeguards

With his dozens of death omens. Randolph listed many safeguards our ancestors contrived. A responsible homemaker never swept floors after dark or let the lamp burn up every bit of its oil. Many kept a red string or a bit of red cloth in the oil reservoir as protection.

🐾 Anyone using a gun was careful not to kick it, lest someone present later die of gunshot (kicking a loaded gun might guarantee that someone died that way immediately!)

🐾 Burning peach wood and transplanting cedars were invitations to death. So were bringing outdoor tools like hoes into the house.

🐾 Among emergency actions one could take to ward off evil if it came near: throw salt in the fire or a handful of feathers. Or quickly tie a series of knots in a string. This latter tactic may be connected to witchcraft, in which great control is thought to lie in tying tight knots at certain times, in certain places.

A Modern Mystery

Working with folklore almost forces vicarious sharing of what others have felt when faced with the inexplicable. Little experiences we might otherwise dismiss take on new significance, when compared with those of our forebears. Here's something my grandmothers would probably have worried with until they had figured out a logical meaning.

It was long after midnight on a silent fall evening. I don't know why I was on the porch at that hour with my dogs, but I will never forget how they rose, almost in unison and looked east with keen interest. In a few seconds I could hear, barely, the sound of an approaching siren. It was hardly recognizable, though, being wrapped, literally, with the voices of dogs. As the siren came closer, more voices joined in, as if every dog along the way was adding its bit. They harmonized in key, pitch, volume and poignancy with those already howling, as if trying to echo exactly the frightful message of all sirens: "Here comes the thing most awful! Death is among us!"

The dogs of our town sounded like a well-practiced choir, whose members had been placed evenly along the siren's route so they could help maintain the strength of its message about shared helplessness and sorrow. As my own pets contributed and the ambulance drew closer, the sound grew more and more chilling, though still beautiful. I'd never heard some of my dogs howl, and the others seldom did. They'd certainly never performed as a quartet before. Here they seemed to be consciously trying to sound as much like the siren as they could, intent on their task, oblivious to me.

When this machine and dog chorus was closest to us, it was terrifying, but as it faded, a feeling of peace flowed in, as if drawn by a restful vacuum. Still I was shaken, my whole being wondering "What was that?" My dogs became silent, though they remained standing or sitting on their haunches, every sense still alert. They listened as the dogs who lived west of us took up their segment of the assignment, listened until nothing remained of the siren-canine duet.

The days and weeks that followed brought no news of a prominent person who'd died in our area, no car wreck or house fire or other tragedy that cost several lives. I never heard that anyone had taken a stolen ambulance for a cross-country joy ride.

What would Aunt Sis and my great-grandmothers have said about this strange concert? I'm sure they'd never have dismissed it as an interesting manifestation of animal behavior with no particular meaning. Those ladies would have figured out why the incident was significant.

Chapter Twenty Four

Missouri Burials

Our ancestors' efforts to placate death by responding correctly to omens continued on when the inevitable happened. Departures of loved ones brought family and community to the brink of another world, so numerous measures were taken to protect those remaining and to show proper respect to the deceased. It would be hard to guess how closely tied our culture actually was and is to cultures in which spirits of the recently dead are believed to be a danger to the living, unless certain gestures are made. It has always been common for the newly bereaved to report seeing the ghost of the person recently lost. Often they insist they've received a message in some other way. This may be one reason why it is assumed that a bereaved person should not be left alone, but should have another living person's bolstering presence or a houseful, as is the case of many ethnic groups.

Here are some of the customs reported by Vance Randolph in his books about the Ozarks and by Karen Rae Mehaffey, in *The After Life*. Randolph said clocks were stopped immediately when someone died because it was believed that if a clock ran down while a corpse lay in the house, another family member would die within the year. Mirrors were covered, lest visitors see their reflection while visiting the house of death; if they did,

they'd not last through the fall. Another immediate action taken was to hang the dead person's bedding and clothing out to air, which notified the neighborhood that death had occurred. There also was the custom of burning the dead person's pillow. Perhaps this was merely an anti-contagion move or perhaps it was something more.

Mehaffey offers a different spin, saying that in cities a wreath on the door and black bunting hung above it and perhaps above windows let passersby know they were near a house of mourning that deserved quiet and respect. Shades and draperies made the interior dark, and mirrors were covered with black. Probably the idea was that it would be offensively frivolous at times of sorrow to be concerned about ones appearance, yet the ritual of mourning dress and conduct was rigid.

Mehaffy says that people who could afford it always had wardrobes of black in storage, ready for funerals. And, of course, deaths within families were more frequent then than now; people were often faced with the need to wear mourning for weeks or months. Some widows — Queen Victoria, for instance — never put their black aside. Elaborate tables of rules existed telling one just how long mourning should be worn and social appearances curtailed. One example from Mehaffey: a second wife should wear half-mourning for three months when the parents of her husband's first wife died!

In Pulaski County, our neighbor, Minnie, dwelt on none of these customs, but she was well acquainted with how the body itself was handled. She said that the first thing done when people thought death had occurred was to hold a mirror to the person's mouth to be sure breathing had totally stopped; they knew from experience that life signs can be subtle. Another test was sticking pins in the flesh; holes closed if the person was still alive. Minnie said that being buried alive was a common fear in her own girlhood and most elders could tell of someone "reviving" after being thought dead. Before we laugh at this, we need to remember that our own media sometimes reports a person awakening in a morgue and living weeks or months longer.

Embalming was not widely available in the early part of last century nor were pronouncements by professionals, because of travel difficulties to rural areas. Anyone whose research involves old publications has seen grisly accounts of exhumed bodies found in attitudes of desperation and casket linings ripped to shreds. Stories also appeared of city families unsealing mausoleums to deposit a casket and finding huddled against the door, remains of the person last laid to rest there. One of Edgar Allen Poe's most famous stories, "The Premature Burial," reviews such cases and discusses the uncertainties in his day about whether death had actually occurred. His plot concerns the elaborate means one man took to be able to summon help from the grave.

Randolph mentions another immediate death task, getting the deceased person's eyes closed for good. Heavy coins were the usual means, and he tells with humor of poor families that had silver dollars kept, with difficulty, just for this purpose through several generations. He refers to bitter quarrels that arose because some families refused to lend their "corpse money."

Washing and dressing the body was done, according to Randolph, by anyone *but* the immediate family. Minnie disagreed, saying women, if physically able, wanted to perform this last intimate service for those they loved. Modest mores of the time counted it a great indignity for the nakedness of the helpless dead to be exposed to eyes which would never have seen them so in life. Mothers particularly wanted to be the ones who had final contact with the lovely little bodies of their children. Others might help by preparing clothing, but made sure that if sewing was done on a shroud, the needle was isolated afterwards because if used to sew for living people, it could bring them harm.

In preparing bodies for burial, people early this century used a device Randolph does not mention, the cooling board. Not every family owned one; perhaps only a few existed in any neighborhood, but would be available to whomever needed them. These were six feet in length or longer and just wide enough to hold a body. Placed across chair backs or from table to other furniture, they put the body at a convenient height for bathing and dressing.

The cooling board might be rough wood with only crude holes or slots punched out, or it might be expensive and nicely finished, decorated with elaborate scrolled openwork. Either way, it helped bodies to lose warmth quickly and stay in the best possible condition for the funeral.

Randolph wrote of interesting things being buried with the dead. He knew of one instance where a silver dollar was placed in a man's mouth. The relative Randolph questioned about it didn't know why and Randolph didn't seem to know either. Ancient people used this means of being sure that their departing loved one could pay Charon, the ferryman who takes souls across the River Styx into the hereafter.

Some individuals, including Belle Starr, Randolph said, left orders for guns to go with them. He knew of one old man who had rifle and pistol — both loaded and cocked — sent with him as far as they could go toward eternity.

Earlier in the twentieth century, funerals were held in the homes; bodies prepared for burial lay in state, usually in the parlor. Mehaffey says that among the wealthy, they often lay in their own bed. But even if a funeral was to be held from church instead of home, a "death watch" was customary in Randolph's hills, in the Gasconade valley familiar to my people, and in cities among the wealthy. Randolph felt that never leaving the body alone had its origins in the need to protect it from wild predators that might seek it out. Some felt that household cats were another hazard; under those sweet purry feline exteriors could lurk demons alert for a chance to desecrate the dead!

But my mother, going often with her own mother to sit up in homes while someone "lay a corpse," saw more practical reasons. One was keeping cold, damp cloths on the body's face and hands to retard discoloration. Another reason for this vigil was to be present if life returned, because of the horror it would be for anyone to regain consciousness in a casket, all alone. My mother said that sitting in the small hours by lamp or candle light, it was easy to imagine chest movement in a body. She many times went closer to be sure.

The main reason for sitting up with bodies, she said, was to spell the family in keeping prayerful company with the deceased for as long as possible, another act of respect and love. The hope was that prayer would make the journey easier for a soul in transit, protecting it from unkind spirits enroute.

Grave digging, usually done by neighbors and slightly removed family members, had its own set of taboos and beliefs. Randolph recorded several. For instance, a pick and shovel, handles crossed, must lie on the dirt waiting to be replaced and all grave diggers must remain until the last shovelful of soil was on the grave, or chance dying within a year.

Even the placement of graves mattered: the head must always be to the West. In our community only a few decades ago, some people were much disturbed by a married couple's decision to have their heads on either side of a joint stone. "This is awful!" someone told me. "She's the only one in the cemetery facing west!" When

I asked why it mattered, she said, "Why Jesus will come from the east at resurrection! Wouldn't you want to rise facing him?"

One custom Lucile Morris Upton spoke of in her Springfield newspaper column many years ago started a lively debate among her readers. That was the practice of leaving graves open overnight, believing anything else was an invitation to disaster. Some people wrote indignantly to say the opposite was true. Since most people wanted a funeral over by noon, gravediggers were under great pressure, and as with so many demanding customs, ways were found to get around it.

An elderly man who worked with his father as community grave digger in Pulaski County early in the 1900s told me they left graves technically unfinished until the day of burial. "I don't remember what was supposed to happen if you didn't," he laughed, "but it was so important to so many people that we'd do all but the last few shovelsful the day before and then get down in the grave and 'finish' on the day of the funeral. We needed to dig the grave as early as we could to be sure it would be ready on time, not delayed by rain or snow or our getting into rocks or frozen ground."

He told of digging in summers so hot they had to work at night by lantern light, which he admitted was a little eerie and a sight passersby turned away from. He dug when it was so cold topsoil was like rock and had to be chopped with an axe into squares that could be lifted off to reach diggable dirt.

In our time, closest relatives sometimes crumble the first handful of dirt into the grave before it is closed, but Randolph wrote that in earlier eras people threw in many different things. Items he named ranged from cornmeal to chicken entrails, and for each there had originally been a reason. Paw paw seeds, for example, were thrown on coffins of murder victims to help bring killers to justice.

Funeral processions had rules too. Because anything causing a halt could mean another member of the family would die soon, horsemen went ahead to make sure all gates were open. To cause delay or worse still, collide with a vehicle in a funeral procession, Randolph said, was as good as suicide.

Fans were important at funerals all year round, for in winter, buildings were often overheated and that, with the emotion of the situation, was conducive to fainting. At one time the bereaved family or funeral director if there was one, provided fans as "favors" for all women attending and the quality of the fan reflected the family's financial status.

Most women, in addition to fans, felt they needed "smelling salts." An aged friend of my mother's gave me the little vial she carried, when young, in order to stay vertical. After more than half a century, the ammonia-soaked pellets still jolted breathing passages and brain into full alert.

One fascinating reversal of superstition leaves us not knowing what to think of our ancestors. A Dixon man who provided the community with a horse-drawn hearse told me that people were always trying to buy his teams. "Just when I got a nice black pair trained the way I wanted and looking nice, someone would ask me to price them. Considering what they thought about other things, you'd expect people to be scared to death of hearse horses, sure they'd take them nowhere but to the grave-yard. But no, their common sense took over in this case. They knew these animals had been trained to behave well at all times, to stand quietly wherever they were supposed to stand, to ignore anything in a crowd that might upset an ordinary horse. And hearse horses were usually pretty, always well cared for, never overworked. They stayed sound into their old age. I sold lots of hearse horses for good prices."

Epilogue

So here we are again at the end of another collection of ghost stories and general puzzlers. Intent has not been to prove anything; doing that is impossible, even when two or more people attest to the same experience. The old saying still prevails: "a man convinced against his will is of his old opinion still."

But it must mean something that so many people are so interested in ghost stories, and that so many have mysterious experiences to share. It must mean something that most readers are more interested in what other lay people have seen and felt, than in what scholars and psychologists tell us about the unexplainable. Or maybe that's only in Missouri, where we prefer hearing testimony and drawing our own conclusions!

And will there be another sequel to my *Missouri Ghosts*? People asked that as soon as this book was underway. There certainly could be; half a file drawer full of good material awaits and dozens more people offered stories than time allowed for interviewing. Most of that data — like what you've just read — has not been published before, or only in local newspapers. If another book materializes, it will again glean rural and small town Missouri. Robbi Courtaway's *Spirits of St. Louis* and Maurice Schwalm's *Mo-Kan Ghosts*, both published in 1999, leave little to say about the state's biggest cities. And Jim Longo has done another book, dealing mainly, again, I understand, with riverside ghosts. Let us all just hope to stay in print as long as Vance Randolph has!

Bibliography

Books

Amorth, Fr. Gabriele, *An Exorcist Tells His Story*, Ignatius Press, 1999.

Bartlett, John, *Bartlett's Familiar Quotations*, Little, Brown, 1955.

Bayliss, Raymond, *Apparitions and Survival of Death*, A Citadel Press Book, 1973, and *Animal Ghosts*, University Books, Inc. 1970.

Brophy, Patrick, *Past Perfect, True Tales of Town and 'Round, Nevada and Vernon County, Missouri*, Vernon County Historical Society, 2000.

Carnahan, Jean, *If Walls Could Talk*, Mansion Preservation Society, State of Missouri, 1999.

Courtaway, Robbi, *Spirits of St. Louis*, Virginia Publishing Company, 2000.

Derendinger, Elaine, Melba Fleck and La Vaughn Miller, *Stories of Howard County, Mo, "The Mother of Counties,"* South Howard County Historical Society, 1999.

Gilbert, Joan, *Missouri Ghosts*, Pebble Publishing, 1997.

John Haden of Virginia, Family Genealogy owned by Joel Haden of Colulmbia, MO.

Hauck, Dennis William, *The National Directory of Haunted Places*, Athanor Press, 1994.

Heitz, Lisa Hefner, *Haunted Kansas*, University of Kansas Press, 1997.

Longo, Jim, *Haunted Odyssey*, 1986, and *Ghosts Along the Mississippi*, 1993, both from St. Ann's Press.

Mehaffey, Karen Rae, *The After-Life, Mourning Rituals and the Mid-Victorians*, Laser Writers Publishing, 1993.

Norman, Michael and Beth Scott, *Haunted Heartland*, Dorset Press, 1985, and *Haunted America*, TOR, 1994 and *Historic Haunted America*, TOR, 1995.

Randolph, Vance, *Ozarks Magic and Folklore*, Columbia University Press, 1947, Dover Facsimile, 1964.

Schwalm, Maurice, *Mo-Kan Ghosts*, Belfry Books, 1999.

Steele, Phillip, *Ozark Tales and Superstition*, Pelican Publishing, 1983.

Walker, Stephen P. Lemp, *The Haunting History*, Lemp Preservation Society, Inc. fifth printing, 1993.

Ward, Frank, *Close Behind Thee, American Ghost Stories*, Whitechapel Productions, 1998.

Woolery, Dr. D. R., *The Grand Old Lady of the Ozarks*, third edition, 1986, privately published.

Magazines
(many of these did not list authors' names)

Blue and Gray, February 13, 1902, "de hag rid hoss".

Columbia Senior Times, "Prominent Citizen Odon Guitar: Columbia's "Little General." October, 1999 by Michelle Windmoeller; "The Dedham Moors Inn," December, 1999 by Harold Holder.

Country Folk Magazine, "The Ghost of Dugan Lane," Autumn, 1994 and "Windyville," April-June, 1996, both by Ronnie Powell.

Discovery, Summer 1987, "An Ozarks Original, Eureka Springs, Arkansas", 1987.

Fate, May 2000, "The City of Victorian Ghosts", Richard D. Seifried.

Ghosts of the Prairie, Summer, 1997, "Haunted Theaters," and "The Ghostly History of the Lemp Mansion in St. Louis," October 1997, by Troy and Amy Taylor.

Life, November, 1980 "Terrifying Tales of Nine Haunted Houses."

Missouri Life, October 1981, "The Haunting Legacy of a St. Louis Brewer," by N. L. Hammen.

Ozarks Mountaineer, July-August, 1985, "Ghosts of the Crescent", Phillip Steele.

The Pacific Spectator, a Journal of Interpretation, Autumn, 1948, "Ghost Life on the Mississippi," Samuel C. Webster.

Rural Missouri, "The House That Time Forgot", December, 1999.

St. Louis magazine, October 1992, "Local Haunts for the Amateur Ghost Hunters."

Newspapers

Columbia Daily Tribune, August through November 1998, four stories about the fate of Confederate Hill, written by Scott Mayes, Sarah Baxter and Leslie Wright.

Columbia Missourian, November 30, 1998, "Video Show To Air Story of Rivercene," Darcy Hines, clip undated, fall of 1993. And, "A Grand Opening For New Nightclub at Haden House," Frannie Biebel.

Kansas City Star, October 29, 1995, "Lurid Tale of Exorcism, more than Halloween Lore," by Diana Aitcheson.

Montgomery County Journal, April 25, 1867 and November 3, 1870, stories about a repeated walk-through and about the dead child who sought help for her mother.

Ozarks Senior Living, October 1997, "The Ghosts in Our House Were Friendly but Clumsy," by Joyce O'Neal.

St Joseph (MO) News-Press/Gazette, issues of October 29, 1989, October 31, 1993 and November 18, 1999 had several stories each about St. Joseph ghosts, some attributed to authors and some not.

St. Louis Post Dispatch, October 26, 1986, "The Ghost of Whittemore House," by Kristine Bertelson; September 7, 1993, "Diary of an Exorcism" by John M. McQuire; November 28, 1999, "Investigation Confirms Rumor About Illinoisan," by Linda Sickler; and January 23, 2000,"Excelsior Springs Attracts Visitors," by Mike Bichlis.

Salem News, undated clipping, "Gentle Spirit Haunts Historic Salem House," Renee J. Raper.

Second 50 Forum, July, 1987, "Ghosts of the Mississippi", by Mary Kimbrough.

Springfield News and Leader, October 28, 1973, "Opulence in the Ozarks," feature with story by Jane Bennett and pictures by Betty Love.

St. Charles Heritage, October, 1994, several unattributed ghost stories.

Up Front, St. Louis, May 1991, story of Johann Kuhschwarz by Deanna Bruno.

The Washington University Medical Alumni Quarterly, October, 1937, excerpt by Robert E. Scheuter from a book by Joseph Nash McDowell.

Other

Manuscripts: "The Ghost at the Holloman Place",
Paul Hinchey, undated.
"The Story of Deadman's Pond",
John D. Harris, 1975.

Video: *The Haunted Hills, Ghost Stories of the Ozarks*,
Phillip Steele/Terry Shirley, Heritage Productions

Newsletters: *The Flashlight* "Victorian Guide to Eureka
Springs since 1880" April, 1999

U. S. Psi Squad, Spring, 1998.

Index

To Order More from MoGho Books

Send the form below to:
MoGho Books, P. O. Box 200, Hallsville, MO
with $18.00 for each copy of **More Missouri Ghosts**
desired. Postage, tax, and handling is included in that
simplified price. (Sorry, no credit card facilities yet.)

Also available from MoGho books is **The Extended
Circle, a Dictionary of Humane Thought**. This 436
page collection of quotations about animals contains the
thoughts of everyone from Minnie Pearl to Abraham
Lincoln, thoughts from all times and all places.
Published in 1985 in England, its discounted prices now
are $12.50 hardback and $9, paperback. This book has
been called "The Animal Lovers' Bible."

Name_____

Address_____

Names and quantities of books_____

_____

_____

To Order More from MoGho Books

Send the form below to:
MoGho Books, P. O. Box 200, Hallsville, MO
with $18.00 for each copy of **More Missouri Ghosts**
desired. Postage, tax, and handling is included in that
simplified price. (Sorry, no credit card facilities yet.)

Also available from MoGho books is **The Extended
Circle, a Dictionary of Humane Thought**. This 436
page collection of quotations about animals contains the
thoughts of everyone from Minnie Pearl to Abraham
Lincoln, thoughts from all times and all places.
Published in 1985 in England, its discounted prices now
are $12.50 hardback and $9, paperback. This book has
been called "The Animal Lovers' Bible."

Name_____

Address_____

Names and quantities of books_____
_____
_____

To Order More from MoGho Books

Send the form below to:
MoGho Books, P. O. Box 200, Hallsville, MO
with $18.00 for each copy of **More Missouri Ghosts** desired. Postage, tax, and handling is included in that simplified price. (Sorry, no credit card facilities yet.)

Also available from MoGho books is **The Extended Circle, a Dictionary of Humane Thought**. This 436 page collection of quotations about animals contains the thoughts of everyone from Minnie Pearl to Abraham Lincoln, thoughts from all times and all places. Published in 1985 in England, its discounted prices now are $12.50 hardback and $9, paperback. This book has been called "The Animal Lovers' Bible."

Name_____

Address_____

Names and quantities of books_____
_____
_____